PRAISE FOR
12 Hours to a *Great* Marriage

"Buy this book NOW before the authors realize how much it's really worth and before they realize how much you'd pay for an easy-to-use guide to a great marriage. It actually makes working on your marriage fun. In fact, it introduces an approach that believes having fun is one of the hallmarks of a successful marriage. You can't beat that. Twelve hours to the relationship of your dreams."

> —**DIANE SOLLEE**, smartmarriages.com, and founder and director of the Coalition for Marriage, Family and Couples Education

"Delivered in a personal and engaging style, the most helpful book yet from the 'dream team' of marriage educators."

> —**WILLIAM J. DOHERTY**, Ph.D., professor, University of Minnesota, and author of *Take Back Your Marriage: Sticking Together in a World That Pulls Us Apart*

"I love this book! It's like hiring your own top-notch relationship coach for twelve hours and getting a lifetime's worth of lessons for creating a loving, lasting marriage. I will heartily recommend this book to the couples in my practice!"

> —**MICHELE WEINER-DAVIS**, author, *The Sex-Starved Marriage* and *Divorce Busting*

"This practical guide to a loving relationship provides such vivid examples of destructive patterns that distressed couples will wonder whether the authors installed a hidden camera in their homes. Tackling difficult issues such as sexuality, interfaith marriages, and forgiveness within the framework of communication skills and conflict resolution makes this book much more than a simple how-to manual."

> —**SHIRLEY P. GLASS**, Ph.D., ABPP, author, *NOT "Just Friends": Protect Your Relationship from Infidelity and Heal the Trauma of Betrayal*

"This book makes lasting love achievable."

> —**JOHN GRAY**, author, *Men Are from Mars, Women Are from Venus*

12 Hours TO A Great Marriage

12 Hours TO A Great Marriage

A Step-by-Step Guide for Making Love Last

Howard J. Markman • Scott M. Stanley
Susan L. Blumberg • Natalie H. Jenkins
Carol Whiteley

JOSSEY-BASS
A Wiley Imprint
www.josseybass.com

Published by Jossey-Bass
A Wiley Imprint
989 Market Street, San Francisco, CA 94103-1741   www.josseybass.com

Readers should be aware that Internet Web sites offered as citations and/or sources for further information may have changed or disappeared between the time this was written and when it is read.

Jossey-Bass books and products are available through most bookstores. To contact Jossey-Bass directly call our Customer Care Department within the U.S. at 800-956-7739, outside the U.S. at 317-572-3986, or fax 317-572-4002.

Jossey-Bass also publishes its books in a variety of electronic formats. Some content that appears in print may not be available in electronic books.

Book design by Suzanne Albertson

Library of Congress Cataloging-in-Publication Data
12 hours to a great marriage : a step-by-step guide for making love last /
Howard J. Markman ... [et al.].
        p. cm.
Includes bibliographical references.
    ISBN 0-7879-6800-5 (alk. paper)
    1. Marriage. 2. Man-woman relationships. I. Title: Twelve hours to a
great marriage. II. Markman, Howard, date.
    HQ734.A13 2003
    646.7'8—dc21

                                                    2003006250
Printed in the United States of America
FIRST EDITION
PB Printing   10 9 8

CONTENTS

Acknowledgments

T he PREP approach, as presented in this book, is built on the foundations of researchers of marriage and family relationships from many fields. In particular, the work of the following individuals has been influential in aspects of our work: Paul Amato, Don Baucom, Steven Beach, Tom Bradbury, Vernon Call, Andy Christensen, Mari Clements, James Cordova, Steven Duck, Wayne Duncan, Norm Epstein, Frank Fincham, Frank Floyd, Peter Fraenkel, Norvelle Glenn, John Gottman, Bernard Guerney, Kurt Hahlweg, Kim Halford, Tim Heaton, Chris Heavey, Amy Holtzwoth-Monroe, Jill Hooley, Ted Huston, Ted Jacob, Neil Jacobson, Matt Johnson, Mike Johnson, Danielle Julian, Ben Karney, Janice Kiecolt-Glaser, Shelle Kraft, Lawrence Kurdek, Doug Leber, Kris Lindahl, Gayla Margolin, Sherrod Miller, Peter Neidig, Steve Nock, Pat Noller, Clifford Notarius, Dan O'Leary, Theodora Ooms, Gerald Patterson, Jane Pearson, Lydia Prado, Mari Jo Renick, Caryl Rusbult, Matt Sanders, Cas Schaap, Ben Silliman, Benard Spilka, Ragnar Storaasli, Kieran Sullivan, Brigit VanWidenfelt, Linda Waite, Robert Weiss, and Ev Worthington. This is only a partial list, for the complete listing would be a chapter unto itself. It is the work of people such as these that has so greatly informed our efforts to help couples.

We also would like to acknowledge those who have worked with us to develop other books for couples based on our approach: David and Claudia Arp, William Bailey, Milt Bryan, Joel Crohn, Pamela Jordan, Janice Levine, Savanna McCain, Daniel Trathen, and Keith Whitfield. Savanna McCain and Daniel Trathen have been making substantial contributions to this body of work for many years now.

We cannot thank the PREP staff enough for their ongoing support in the effort to reach couples with evidence-based materials. Our staff has brought great drive, energy, and creativity to the task of disseminating this approach to couples around the world. Having solid material that can help couples is one thing; getting it to couples—and those who work to help couples—is quite another, and our staff makes this happen. Many staff members have helped us over the years, and this time we'd like to specifically acknowledge the work of our current staff, including Nita Wassenaar, Sheryl Haddock, Jennifer Foran—a more talented and kind group you could not find.

Over the years, we've been excited to work with all the branches of our U.S. armed forces. We've had the good fortune to connect over the years with many people who have supported us in meaningful ways as our work has developed, including Bill Coffin and his colleagues in the U.S. Navy: Kathryn Barnard, Michael Cassidy, Lyn Davis, Robert Emde, Scott Halford, Richard Hunt, and Swanee Hunt. All deserve our thanks for their encouragement in expanding our reach to meeting the needs of couples. Bill Coffin, in particular, has been a true visionary in his efforts to support prevention efforts for building strong marriages in both military and civilian communities. He has been an especially potent force in helping bring evidence-based materials to couples throughout the U.S. military services, beginning with the U.S. Navy in the early 1990s. He saw a need and looked for ways to meet it.

Another person who deserves special notice—and who has our deep respect—is Chaplain Glen Bloomstrom of the U.S. Army. Glen has been a tireless leader in bringing PREP training to Army families through the work of the chaplain corps. In the Army, Navy, and Air Force, we've been privileged to get to know and work with hundreds of chaplains who go the extra mile in reaching and supporting the lives of these fine men and women. We've also been delighted to work with Family Advocacy, a group that works hard to help military couples prevent domestic violence in all branches of the service.

These are just a few of the people in our armed forces who have put the military services on the cutting edge of efforts to prevent marital distress and strengthen families. The military does not get nearly the credit it deserves for all these efforts, and we believe they are far ahead of the curve in terms of helping young couples.

We cannot thank our friend Gary Smalley enough for his support and encouragement in recent years. It is a rare and humble man who so freely helps others in the same field in which he works. Gary is such a man, and we are inspired by his love and his work. We also thank Diane Sollee for her national efforts to put marriage education on the map. In her development of the Smart Marriages conference, she has provided a place for people from widely divergent backgrounds to join together and share knowledge, expertise, and experiences with the common goal of helping build stronger, happier, and more stable marriages. She is a good friend who shares our passion for prevention.

As we've conducted research on this approach over the years, we have been assisted by bright and energetic research assistants and consultants. The number of these people with whom we've been privileged to work has grown so very large that their names can't be listed here, but we deeply thank all these folks who have been so important in our work.

Most of the research reported in this book has been supported over the years by the University of Denver; the National Institute of Mental Health: Division of Services and Intervention Research, Adult and Geriatric Treatment and Prevention Branch, Grant 5-RO1-MH35525-12, "The Long-term Effects of Premarital Intervention"; and the National Science Foundation. We are grateful for the support from these institutions; it has enabled us to develop the research basis for the program presented in this book. The emphasis in our book on preventing problems before they develop—in addition to treating them—is one that has been shared by the National Institute of Mental Health, and we express our gratitude for its support of our research program on the possibilities of preventing divorce and marital distress.

We would also like to acknowledge the collaborative spirit and contributions of the National Institute of Mental Health's Family Research Consortium 3, of which Howard was a member. We thank the following bright, talented, and committed researchers, colleagues, and friends for their support, insights, and help in shaping our vision of family research: Mark Appelbaum, Jeannie Brooks-Gunn, Linda Burton, Ana Marie Caucé, Lindsay Chase-Landsdale, Rand Conger, Martha Cox, Marion Forgatch, Della Hand, Stuart Hauser, and Ron Kessler.

Our editor at Jossey-Bass, Alan Rinzler, has worked with us on many books now. His support and wisdom throughout have been so deeply appreciated by us.

Alan has been not only a stellar editor but an "operations manager" par excellence. He and his terrific staff have added significantly to the quality of this book. We all thank Alan for his support, dedication, patience, sense of humor, and leadership. In addition to Alan, we want to thank Alan's staff at Jossey-Bass, including Carol Hartland, Seth Schwartz, Catherine Craddock, Erin Jow, Jennifer Wenzel, Lasell Whipple, Karen Warner, Paula Goldstein, and copyeditor Michele Jones, for their support and expertise during this process.

We would like to acknowledge the role that our clients and seminar participants have played in shaping the ideas and case histories presented in the book. We have disguised their identities in the vignettes through the use of composites and detail changes. Nevertheless, the stories told by many couples over the years are often so strikingly similar that the themes in the case histories we present will speak to a variety of people. We can all learn from each other.

Carol would also like to thank her agent, Carol Susan Roth, of Carol Susan Roth Literary, for her expertise and support and for the opportunity to work with the great team at PREP and contribute to this book. She also sends big thanks to her friend and business partner Murray Suid, for his advice, generosity, and inspiration.

Howard would also like to thank his parents, Claire and Arnold, for their comments on the chapters and Mat for his research on baseball and marriage.

Finally, we want to express our deep sense of appreciation for the couples and families who have shared their lives with us in our various research projects. Over the years, these couples have opened their hearts and their relationships to our interviewers and video cameras. They have shared their struggles and successes, and we hope that the knowledge presented in this book represents some small compensation to these couples, without whom the book could never have been written.

Howard J. Markman
Scott M. Stanley
Susan L. Blumberg
Natalie H. Jenkins
Carol Whiteley

12 Hours TO A Great Marriage

To Janine, Mat, Leah, Mark, Mom and Dad—your love, acceptance, and support nourish me every day and are appreciated more than you all know.
—HJM

To Nancy, Kyle, and Luke, with all my love
—SMS

To my parents, for their love and support
To Aviva and Natan, for bringing such joy into my life
To Lewis, always
—SLB

Shawn—As I notice the gray in your hair I realize we really are "growing old together." For over twenty years we've not merely grown older, but we continue to learn how to love. Thank you for growing older and wiser with me.
—NHJ

To Mark, the most wonderful son in the world, and to Trina, Dad, Joan, and Bob—you're the best.
—CW

INTRODUCTION:
STEPPING UP TO THE PLATE

If someone asked you what you wanted most out of life, what would you say? One of the deepest longings of people everywhere is to have a great relationship, especially in the form of a great marriage. No matter what their background, age, or circumstances, most adults on the planet yearn for the love, fun, acceptance, and deep connection that can come from a happy, lifelong relationship.

Do you dream of having a great marriage? It's a good dream to have. A great, forever marriage is a wonderful thing to be part of, and can enrich your life. The question is, though, how do you turn your dream into reality?

This book was written to help you bring your dream closer. In it we've condensed everything we've learned from our 25 years of marital research and experience into a 12-hour program that will help you develop and protect a loving relationship. Whether you are happily married and want to stay that way, having issues you'd like help with, or planning to marry and want to know how to preserve all the great things about your relationship, the information in this book can help you make it happen.

Just 12 hours to a great marriage? We understand if you're a little skeptical. We want to say right up front that it's going to take more than 12 hours to develop a happy, deeply satisfying, loving, lasting marriage. In fact, you and your partner are going to have to commit to a lifetime of teamwork to have the relationship you really want. But the approximately 12 hours it takes to read this book and do the exercises can put you well on your way to making your dream come true.

If you're like most people, though, it might be hard for you to find even 12 hours to devote to this program. Life just keeps getting busier and busier. But if you want to celebrate your 50th wedding anniversary some day, carving out 12 hours now to help you make sure those 50 years are good ones doesn't seem like too much to ask.

To help you out, we've set things up so you don't have to find the 12 hours all at once. We've organized this book so you can work on its easy-to-understand, proven program just one hour at a time, one chapter at a time. We think you'll find each hour so full of real help and inspiration that you'll make the time to do all 12 hours soon. But you don't have to stay up all night or go without food to get under way.

THINKING IN NEW WAYS

Taking it an hour at a time is a wonderful way to start creating your dream partnership. So is thinking about marriage in a way you've probably never thought about it before—like (are you ready?) a great game of baseball!

Baseball? Baseball and marriage? Yes. Definitely. After working with thousands of couples to improve their relationships and prevent divorce, we think a good game of baseball has a whole lot in common with marriage. Here's what we've found they have in common:

- To succeed, you've got to work as a team.
- Each player must cover his or her own position.
- You've got to play by the rules.
- Good strategy can make the difference between winning and losing.
- All players need to keep up their skills.
- It's possible to strike out, but with hard work and determination you can hit a home run.
- Unsportsmanlike behavior can get you benched or thrown out.
- Sometimes you have to sacrifice.
- You're supposed to have a good time.
- There's no spitting allowed. (OK, we *wish* there were no spitting allowed.)

Do you see what we mean? Marriage and baseball really do have a lot in common. So as you work with this program, we suggest you think of baseball as a helpful comparison. By stepping up to the plate, digging in, and following the proven strategies you're going to learn here, your team can have a championship season.

WHY CAN IT BE HARD TO MAKE LOVE LAST?

Experts often tell us that it's easy to fall in love but hard to stay there. But why should it be hard if lifelong love is what we desire?

The answer is that, since World War II, the institution of marriage has changed enormously. Before that time, the divorce rate was low: only adultery and abandonment were reasons to end a marriage. Men and women also had similar expectations about the roles they would play and the way they'd raise their family.

Today, things are much different. Women's roles have changed and expanded. People are more mobile, and much less likely to live near family or friends. And expectations for romance and passion have skyrocketed. For many people, there's a big gap between what they have and what they think they should have.

It's also gotten easier to end a marriage. That's good when the marriage is destructive. But it has also caused couples to believe that no marriage works well for the long term, so their marriage must be hopeless too.

Considering all these changes, it's not hard to see why many couples don't achieve the happy, committed marriage they long for.

What is the impact of not having these deep longings met in marriage? For many couples, it means feeling stressed, overwhelmed, and unsure. It also means that, to handle all the new choices and new issues marriage now involves, partners have to negotiate with each other. And the way they handle conflict and differences—part of *all* relationships—has a huge effect on the state of their marriage and the survival of their happiness. In other words, because conflict in any long-term relationship is inevitable, you have to figure out how to manage disagreements and solve problems in a way that protects and preserves your love.

WE'RE GOING TO COACH YOU

In our clinical practices, we've seen many once-happy couples ruin their marriage by fighting in destructive ways. We've also heard them say that they wished they'd learned what we're teaching in this program much earlier in their lives.

Although nearly half of all marriages today end in divorce, yours doesn't have to be one of them. If you use the research-based, field-tested marriage enhancement strategies in this book, you *can* prevent divorce. You *can* increase your happiness.

So think of this book, and us, as your coach. We're going to help you develop your relationship skills, deepen your motivation, and improve your chances of having a happier and richer life with your partner, now and in the future.

OUR WINNING PROGRAM

Just what is this book based on? It's based on a program called PREP®, which stands for the Prevention and Relationship Enhancement Program. We developed PREP after years of in-depth research to show engaged and married couples how to build strong and happy marriages. We've used it to train, counsel, and coach thousands of couples in workshops and seminars over the years, most often through a 12-hour program like the one featured here. Our program has helped couples learn the skills and attitudes that our research shows lead to good relationships, and now we want to help you.

PREP's track record is great: we've helped many couples build their friendship, enhance their commitment, boost their fun, and reduce the negatives that can damage closeness. Because they work so well, our materials are used all around the world. Here in the United States, they're used in community settings, by government agencies, in religious institutions, and throughout the branches of the U.S. military. We're certain they're so successful because they're based on sound research findings from many respected social scientists as well as the continuing research we conduct at the Center for Marital and Family Studies at the University of Denver. They offer simple, straightforward knowledge that you can use to make a difference in your marriage.

Our approach isn't magic. And it isn't therapy or counseling. It's a program that tells you about, and has you practice, a number of simple, effective strategies to develop and protect the love and happiness you want in your relationship. It's a program to help you better your marriage and prevent divorce.

FOUR HALLMARKS OF A GREAT MARRIAGE

Research has shown that the happiest, most deeply contented couples have four things in common, though they may demonstrate them in different ways:

1. They share friendship and love in many ways.
2. They treat each other with kindness and respect.
3. Both partners do their own part.
4. They're committed to staying together, even when it's no bed of roses.

We'll talk more about these ideas in Hours 1 through 12. But here, in a nutshell, is a bit about each.

Your Field of Dreams _____

Remember the movie *Field of Dreams?* In it Kevin Costner plays a husband and father who is moved by mysterious forces to build a baseball field in Iowa. Even if you haven't seen the movie, you may remember the line, "If you build it, they will come." One way we summarize the four hallmarks of a great marriage is by using a baseball field. At first base, we have protecting and sharing friendship and love. Second base is treating each other respectfully when dealing with conflict. Third base is commitment to your marriage—keeping your relationship in first place. At the pitcher's mound is the centerpiece: doing your own part. If you build your field of dreams, you will always be "safe at home."

Sharing Friendship and Love

When we ask people what they want in a lifelong mate, they often say, "A best friend." Most of us long for a partner who will love us and accept us no matter what.

Friendship is essential to a great marriage. In fact, friendship sustains marriage as much as passion does—maybe more. Romantic passion is wonderful, and later in the book we'll give you lots of ways to keep it alive. But there is probably no better way to keep love strong in your marriage than through friendship.

Treating Your Partner with Kindness and Respect

All of us want to be honored and treated well—especially by our partner. But in reality most of us honor least the ones we love the most. When we get mad or frustrated or disappointed, we often take it out on the person closest to us. (We see you nodding!) And our research shows that couples who put each other down and are hostile to each other are the most likely to develop serious problems.

Problems are going to come up in every marriage. That's something you can count on. But when conflicts come up between the two of you, you don't have to react to them with anger or disrespect. And they don't have to put your marriage at risk. The approaches we teach in this book will show you how to prevent or stop destructive ways of handling conflict. They'll also show you how to solve problems with kindness, generosity, and good will—without your being afraid to say what you really think or worry about what might happen.

In other words, our methods for handling conflict should make you feel emotionally and physically safe—and that's essential for having a deeply connected, loving relationship.

Knowing and Doing Your Part

To give your marriage the best chance to succeed, each of you needs to work on your part of the relationship. For example, if you think your spouse is being unfair to you, instead of yelling or doing something unfair back, you should do the most constructive thing you can think of. Your partner's poor behavior mustn't keep you from doing your all for the team—unless you're constantly being victimized. Then you need to seek out other help. (See Getting More Help When There Are Serious Problems at the end of the book.)

Your partner's bad behavior also shouldn't justify bad behavior of your own. Far too often people feel justified hurting their loved ones because they feel hurt themselves.

Because your team is made up of two individuals, each of you will have the most control over your relationship by controlling your own thoughts and actions within it. But if you think you have to understand your behavior before you can control it, don't worry. Although it can be good to know why you do the things you do, you don't have to understand it completely right now.

Instead, you can start by being the best friend and partner you can be and acting in a loving way. Then, as you learn more, you can show your love in even more effective ways. Work to identify and decrease negative behaviors and increase positive ones. And remember that one part of loving well is accepting your partner for who he or she is.

The quizzes and exercises in each hour will help you learn to do your part as well as how to work together better as a team. We'll also give you advice on things that are best done together.

Three Important Ways to Do Your Part

1. Regularly do things that will please your partner. It can be as simple as rubbing her back after a long day at her desk, if that's something you know she enjoys. Or it can be surprising him with tickets—for both of you—to see his favorite team's next home game.

2. Let negative or annoying comments roll off you. If something needs to be dealt with, do it when both of you are calm and you can discuss it in a constructive way.

3. Be the best person you can be. Take responsibility for your own issues, personal growth, appearance, and health. Make the effort to take good care of yourself and improve yourself, for your own sake and the sake of your marriage.

Committing to Staying Together

When they marry, many couples think mainly about the here and now—the wedding, the honeymoon, setting up house. But marriage can and should last a lifetime. (Remember that line about "till death do us part"?) So PREP not only shows you how to change things for the better now but also helps you build a strong relationship for the long term. Our studies show that couples who do the best over the long term think and act in terms of lifelong love.

That means they're committed. And commitment makes some wonderful things happen. When you commit yourself to your marriage, you let your partner know that he or she can count on you—no matter what. That understanding brings you both a great sense of safety. It also brings a sense of permanence. That feeling of permanence—knowing that no matter what is said or done, it won't destroy the relationship—goes a long way to solving relationship problems.

As we take you through the program, we'll give you lots of suggestions for creating that sense of safety and permanence. We'll also encourage you to develop and take great care of the vision of your future together.

THE BENEFITS OF A LASTING MARRIAGE

Although many of you may be reading this book to learn how to sustain an already good marriage, some of you may be reading it because you're experiencing pain.

Some marriages are destructive or even dangerous. Many others are not destructive, but one or both partners are in pain because they've drifted very far apart. If your marriage is physically dangerous, we don't have the advice that will make it safe. For that, we urge you to seek out a person who specializes in helping those in danger get to safety. But if you want to turn a drifting marriage around, much of our advice will be crucial. If the seed of hope is still there, you and your partner can use it to do amazing things together.

But why should you put in the effort? Because the benefits of a strong, lasting marriage are great, and the effects of divorce can be devastating:

1. Children, on average, do best when they're raised by two loving parents. But divorce can have lasting negative effects on children. Children of divorce—especially from families in which the parents fell out of love and the children didn't see the split coming—are more likely to find it hard to have close relationships as adults. They're also at greater risk for dropping out of high school, becoming pregnant in their teens, having mental health problems, and living in poverty.

But all children of divorce aren't doomed. Many do quite well. However, the odds that children will experience negative outcomes sometime in their lives go up with divorce.

It's unclear what effects divorce has on children whose parents have chronic, high levels of conflict, because conflict, in itself, is so damaging to children. Although children from divorced families are at increased risk compared to children raised by parents who get along well, children could be even worse off in life if instead of divorce they have to endure years of nasty conflicts between their parents. If you have children, the best thing you can do for them is also the best thing you can do for yourself and your partner: work to make your marriage strong and happy.

2. People who remain happily married tend to be happier in life and be healthier and live longer than other people. Ongoing marital

strife can literally make you sick, making you more likely to suffer from a variety of physical and mental health problems over time.

3. Long-term married couples are the most likely to be financially secure. In contrast, divorce can cause financial distress and, sometimes, disaster. Many divorced couples who lived comfortably when they were married can find themselves living at a much lower income level, perhaps even ending up in or near poverty.

If your marriage has become painful and difficult, we can't promise that you can turn it around. But we can tell you that many couples have. In fact, a recent survey showed that 34 percent of married people had been so unhappy at one point in their marriage that they'd thought about divorce. But 92 percent of those people said they were glad they had stayed and worked things out. You *can* turn things around, and our strategies have helped many couples do just that.

IT'S YOUR TURN AT BAT

Even without our telling you, you probably know that marital unhappiness and divorce can cause great pain and damage. If you've been reading this introduction, you also know that we think it's possible to prevent divorce and be part of a happy and deeply committed relationship.

Should you work on the program on your own, or is it better to do it with your partner? The answer is, both ways work well. If you're reading this book by yourself, you'll find powerful ideas for helping your marriage individually. If you're working with your partner as a couple, you'll also find great suggestions for ways that both of you can take responsibility. If you are working as a couple, you and your partner may want to begin by agreeing to the following:

- You will work on your relationship as a team.
- You will not fight destructively during the course of the program.
- You will follow the program because you both want the relationship to work.

- You will keep fun and friendship in your partnership.
- You will do your part.
- You will try hard to make your partner feel safe.
- You will not say things that threaten the security of your marriage.
- You will focus on what you put into your relationship rather than what you get out of it.

Whether you're looking to strengthen your marriage on your own or with your partner, we're certain that the strategies we're about to teach you will help you think and act in ways that can turn your "I do's" into "We can."

Are you ready to get started? Let's go!

HEADING FOR HOME

To help you create a lasting love, we've divided this book into 12 chapters based on the 12-hour program we provide to many couples in our workshops. These chapters are grouped into four parts. Each part focuses on one of the PREP keys to success: handling conflict, making positive connections, forgiving, and making a long-term commitment.

Part One: Getting to First

Part One focuses on managing conflict—essential for a smooth playing field. Here you'll learn that although many couples think it's their differences and disagreements that cause the big problems in their relationship, it's really *how they handle* those differences that's important.

Part One teaches you a simple way to handle relationship problems. It also alerts you to the major risks to your relationship and the danger signs to watch out for. Part One also covers the different (sometimes amazingly different!) ways that men and women handle conflict. And we provide specific techniques you can use right away to stop negative behavior patterns and talk without fighting. In addition we'll show you how everyday problems often cover deeper issues—

and how to deal with both. We end the section by giving you a set of steps to use to solve problems, plus six simple ground rules that will let you solve problems without damaging your relationship.

Part Two: Reaching Second

In Part Two you'll learn how important fun and sex are to the health and happiness of your marriage. If you've lost that loving feeling, or want to make it even stronger, the chapters in this section will give you ways to rediscover and deepen it. We'll help you find the time to have fun together and keep conflict from ruining your party, and we'll even suggest activities if you're at a loss for enjoyable things to do. We'll also tell you how you can keep anxiety and conflict out of your physical relationship and how to talk about sex without fear.

Our research has shown that the positive connections you make through fun and sex will do much to strengthen your marriage. We've also found that talking about and building your core beliefs can also improve your connection, so we've included that information as well. Core beliefs can and do involve religious beliefs. But they also include the life-shaping ethics and ideals that people hold—such as the principles that guide the right way to behave.

In Part Two we'll give you specific ideas for enhancing your connections through community involvement. If you and your partner don't share the same religion or worldview, we'll show you how you can keep your differences from damaging your relationship.

Part Three: Rounding Third

In Parts One and Two we talk about what you can do right now to get your marriage on the move. In Part Three we give you ideas that can help it go the distance.

Part Three discusses two issues that are key to a long-term happy marriage: expectations and forgiveness. Expectations—what we believe is going to happen—affect everything, from who's going to take out the garbage to what makes an enjoyable day. Our expectations come from our background and our experiences. Some are explicit and talked about publicly, some are assumed and never communicated out loud.

But what if you and your partner have hugely different expectations? We'll show you how to be aware of expectations, be reasonable and clear about what you expect, and meet your partner's expectations even if they're not your own.

Being in a relationship means you can get hurt from time to time. And when you get hurt, you may feel like striking back—or withdrawing, or denying there's a problem, or holding it against your partner. None of that helps. In fact, they can all make things worse. What does help, as we've seen time after time, is forgiving. Couples who forgive each other not only get over both minor and major hurts but also move forward—happily and together. We'll give you a step-by-step method for working toward forgiveness and making it a rewarding part of your life.

Part Four: Safe at Home

In the last part we focus on two things that will keep your marriage strong and secure for the long term: friendship and commitment. Although sex and passion are definitely important, we've learned that deep friendship between partners will help them go the distance. But being a friend can sometimes be hard, when you're also a lover, mother or father, PTA president, office manager, and dinner maker. So we give you powerful techniques for renewing, deepening, and protecting friendship in your marriage.

Commitment is one of the most important parts of this program. That's because couples need to believe that their relationship will last forever if they are going to take risks, open up to their partner, and put in the effort that will get them around the bases. We'll tell you what other couples do to develop a sense of "us." We'll also give you ways to dedicate yourselves to your shared future.

THE BEST WAY TO USE THIS BOOK

Each chapter in this book should take about an hour to read, take the quiz, and do the exercises. If you're reading this book as a couple, either out loud or taking turns, we encourage you both to read each chapter before doing the exercises. A key part of the program is learning and working as a team. Moving through it together will give you lots of chances to talk about the information as well as put it into practice.

But what if you're all set to read the book and start using the techniques, and your partner doesn't want to? We encourage you to talk with your fiancé or spouse about how marriage is a partnership—there are two of you in it—and that successful partnerships need both partners to participate. It's much more likely that your marriage will be sweet if both of you work to make it that way. You should also point out that our program is based on research and the experiences of successful couples, and ask your partner to read the section "Our Winning Program," on page 4.

If your partner isn't interested in reading and using the book, take heart. You can still do the program on your own and see great results. Each chapter includes a quiz to do on your own, a chance to write about your reaction to the information, and exercises that are relevant to your situation. What *you* learn and put into practice will have a positive effect on your relationship, because when one partner makes a change, the partnership changes. What you do on your own can bring about a happier marriage for both of you.

Once you're ready to start, we encourage you to suit up with confidence. If you're sure you're headed for divorce court and that nothing can help, you may very well end up there. Or if you think you've already achieved a good marriage but that a great one is out of reach, you may stay right where you are.

The good news is that many couples who follow this program have found lasting love and happiness in a deeply committed relationship. If you think you can, you can do it too. Although we make no promises, we believe that by using the skills you'll learn here, you will greatly increase your chances of not only staying together but staying joyously together.

We're rooting for the home team.

PART I

GETTING TO FIRST

Welcome to the start of our 12-hour program! We hope that the many ideas it contains will help you make your marriage everything you've hoped it would be. Our goal is to show you new and effective ways to develop and preserve a loving, lasting relationship.

Before you begin, take a few minutes to read the Introduction to this book, Stepping Up to the Plate. Those pages will tell you quickly about the approach we use and why it works. If you can't read the entire section, please be sure to read at least "It's Your Turn at Bat," "Heading for Home," and "The Best Way to Use This Book." There you'll find suggestions for things you can do to make sure this program benefits you the most.

Because you've decided to read this book, we're assuming you want to make your relationship a happy, secure, and fulfilling one by using the newest research-based, easy-to-use approach. So we want to tell you right now that, more than anything else, how you and your partner treat each other is key to that goal. To get you started in the right direction, the first hour of our program starts by identifying negative ways of talking. That may seem like the wrong way to begin a chapter called Taking a Positive Approach. But because negatives can quickly erode all the great, positive things in your marriage, we want to let you know right away the negative patterns to avoid. Then you can continue—with a positive outlook—on the road to happiness.

Taking a Positive Attitude

How many times have we heard this story?

Jack and Jennifer meet.

They're attracted to each other, and they start to go out.

They fall in love. There's excitement. There's heat.

They get married.

Problems happen—they always do.

Jack and Jennifer stop doing the things that made them want to be together in the first place. They have less fun. They stop talking as friends. They argue a lot.

One or both of them starts to associate the other with pain and stress rather than with support and fun.

The relationship falls apart. Jack and Jennifer forget why they ever wanted to marry.

Jack and Jennifer divorce. Or they don't divorce, but stay very unhappily married.

Couples whose relationship follows this path are usually couples who don't handle conflict well. But conflict, or differences, are part of every relationship. So what can you do to keep the conflict in your relationship from destroying it?

Although there are a number of things that can't be changed that can put conflict in your marriage and put you at risk for divorce, the way you and your spouse handle conflict *can* change and improve.

Risks That Often Can't Be Changed

- Having a personality that reacts defensively to problems and disappointments
- Having divorced parents
- Living together before getting married
- Having been divorced
- Having children from an earlier marriage
- Having different religious backgrounds
- Getting married at a very young age
- Knowing each other for only a short time before getting married
- Having serious money problems
- Experiencing racism often

Although studies show that couples who have one or more of these factors are at increased risk for divorce, many couples who live with such risks have developed very wonderful marriages. Still, if you have some of these risk factors, it's best to acknowledge they exist and understand how they might be affecting your relationship. The approach explained in this book has been shown to help couples not only understand these complex issues but also learn how to counter their negative effects.

Risks That Can Be Changed

- Having negative styles of talking and arguing (for example, putting each other down, refusing to talk, or yelling)
- Having a hard time communicating, especially when you disagree
- Not being able to handle disagreements as a team
- Having unrealistic beliefs about marriage
- Having different ideas about important things
- Not being completely committed to each other for the long term

All these risk factors can damage your relationship. Research shows they're some of the strongest predictors of misery in marriage and divorce. But by learning how to live with them and handle conflict well, your marriage can definitely move beyond them and be a great one.

If some of these risks are part of your relationship (see the quiz on the next page for figuring this out), we'll show you how to lower them. If your risk isn't high, we'll show you how to keep it that way.

GETTING UNDER WAY

This hour focuses on several issues involved in handling conflict. In it you'll learn about the four main ways couples let conflict eat away at all the good feeling between them. We start by talking about conflict because, if it's handled badly, it can quickly kill a marriage. So we tell you how to recognize when you're handling conflict negatively and stop it in its tracks. The rest of Part One—Hours 2, 3, 4, and 5—will give you additional important information about handling conflict. It will also tell you about the first steps to take to create a great marriage and protect your love.

Starting Out Right

Research shows that how a couple starts talking about an issue determines how the talk will go. If you start out angry, the whole talk is liable to be angry. If you start calmly and positively, the conversation most likely will continue that way. John Gottman, a colleague in the marriage enhancement field, encourages using what he calls the "gentle start-up." By bringing up concerns directly but gently, you can keep your talks both comfortable and constructive.

FOUR PATTERNS TO PREVENT OR CHANGE

After years of research and listening to thousands of couples discuss their problems, we've found four main patterns that couples can fall into if they don't handle conflict well:

1. Escalation
2. Invalidation
3. Negative interpretations
4. Withdrawal

These negative patterns are common, and they can tear your marriage apart. And although they're not the only patterns that trouble couples, they threaten the bond that holds you and your partner together and that, over time, can lead to unhappiness and, in many cases, divorce. In fact, research has shown that negative patterns and behaviors have a much stronger effect on marriage than the positive things.

That's the bad news. The good news is that all of these negative patterns can be changed to positive ones.

RELATIONSHIP QUIZ

Before we start telling you about the harmful patterns, we want you to think about the patterns in your own relationship. To help you do that, please answer the seven questions that follow, which were developed as part of a research project we participated in with our colleague Gary Smalley. If both you and your partner answer the questions, you can choose whether or not to share your answers with each other. Sharing your total scores might be useful to get a sense of how each of you views your marriage at this point.

Answer each question as it applies to your relationship, using this scale: 1 = Almost never or never; 2 = Once in a while; 3 = Often.

Once you've taken the quiz, add up your score. Then look for what it means in the explanation that follows.

_____ Little arguments escalate into big fights with accusations, criticism, name-calling, or bringing up past hurts.

_____ My partner criticizes or belittles my opinions, feelings, or desires.

_____ My partner seems to view my words or actions more negatively than I mean them to be.

_____ When we have a problem to solve, it's like we're on opposite teams.

_____ I hold back from telling my partner what I really think and feel.

_____ I feel lonely in this relationship.

_____ When we argue, one of us withdraws, that is, doesn't want to talk about it any more or leaves the room.

CHECK OUT YOUR SCORE

7–11

If you scored between 7 and 11, your relationship probably is in very good shape, at least in the way you handle conflict. But relationships don't stand still. Even if everything is good now, it may be an excellent time to learn how to make your marriage even better and prevent problems from developing.

12–16

A score in this range means you need to be careful. Although you may be happy now, there's the possibility of getting into patterns that can hurt your relationship. Take action now to protect your love.

17–21

If you scored in this range, you need to stop and think about where you're headed. Patterns are in place that put your relationship at risk. It's important to stop those patterns immediately and improve your partnership.

If you discover that some of the negative patterns we describe have already taken root in your relationship, don't worry. We'll show you how to get out of them. If they haven't turned up, we'll show you how to keep them away.

Pattern 1: Escalation

Sometimes when couples talk about an issue, they start out talking pretty calmly. One person says something, the other responds. But then the back-and-forth turns nasty. Someone says something. The other person gets upset and says something unkind or negative back. Pretty soon the talk is full of anger and hurtful comments to and about each other. Voices get louder and emotions get more intense. The calm discussion escalates to a dangerous level.

Almost all couples argue heatedly at times. But when anger and frustration turn to contempt for the other person, couples can do a huge amount of damage.

Here's an example of a major escalation.

JOHN: *(coming home from work and tripping over a toy truck at the front door)* Tiffany, can't you ever get the kids to put away their toys?

TIFFANY: *(exhausted)* Like I have nothing else to do. And like you always clean up after yourself.

JOHN: *(getting upset)* Oh, of course, this is my fault. I forgot you're always right and I'm always wrong.

TIFFANY: *(getting upset too, and becoming sarcastic)* Well, at least you've got that part right.

JOHN: *(increasing the intensity)* Thanks for the support. You know, I don't even know why I stay with you. You're always tearing me down.

TIFFANY: Then maybe you shouldn't stay with me. You wouldn't be tripping over the kids' toys somewhere else.

JOHN: You're right again. Maybe I'll move out.

What happened here is that John and Tiffany started to talk about the everyday problem of kids' not putting away their toys, and ended up threatening each other with ending their relationship. Their talk spun out of control because they didn't know how to keep it constructive and how to work on the issue as a team. They were frustrated, tired, and stressed, and both had something to say. But they ended up hurting each other instead of hearing each other.

Partners can say incredibly horrible things to each other during an escalating argument—things they don't really mean or feel. But once the cruel words are said, they can't be taken back. They may eventually be forgiven, but it's much better not to say them in the first place.

Well, you may be thinking, my partner and I don't fight like that. We don't yell or purposely say hurtful things. So it looks like the problem of escalation doesn't apply to us.

Even if you and your spouse don't have shouting matches, you may be talking about issues by returning a negative comment with a negative comment. And that's a subtle form of escalation. Our research shows that even subtle patterns of escalation can lead to divorce.

Here's an example of a subtle form of escalation.

> MARYANNE: Kenny, did you take out the garbage?
>
> KENNY: I thought you said you'd do it.
>
> MARYANNE: No, that's your job.
>
> KENNY: No, you said you'd do it.
>
> MARYANNE: No, I didn't, and I'm not going to.
>
> KENNY: *(under his breath)* Great, thanks a lot.

Does this sound familiar? Although the argument doesn't seem like much compared to the one John and Tiffany had, the couple is still trading negative comments. They are still pointing fingers. And the intensity increased. Seemingly small arguments like this can take a toll on your marriage—especially if you keep having them. Negative, escalating discussions can chip away at the good things you share and knock your team right out of the league.

De-Escalating

To stop escalating talks in their tracks, you need to know when they're happening. As soon as one partner makes a negative, hurtful comment and it's answered in a similar way by the other partner, you can be pretty sure the conversation is starting to spiral out of control. To stop it before it flies off, there are three main things you and your partner should do:

1. Soften your tone—change the way you're speaking from harsh to calm and kind.
2. Hear and acknowledge your partner's point of view.
3. Give up the need to win. Or, if you just can't, call a Time Out (see page 44) and come back to the issue at a later time.

Softening your tone means backing off, being more pleasant, and being less defensive. Acknowledging your partner's point of view means that you really hear what he or she is saying. Giving up the need to win is just that—and understanding that when you win an argument through escalation, your partner and your partnership lose. All these techniques will keep you from letting a problem turn into a damaging fight. They'll also help you work on the problem as a team.

Let's look again at the painful escalation between John and Tiffany. If one or both of them had realized right away that their comments were getting increasingly hurtful, and if they had started to treat each other with kindness instead of anger, their discussion could have gone like this:

> JOHN: *(coming home from work and tripping over a toy truck at the front door)* Tiffany, can't you ever get the kids to put away their toys?
>
> TIFFANY: *(exhausted and annoyed)* Like I have nothing else to do. And like you always clean up after yourself.
>
> JOHN: *(softening his tone)* I guess you're pretty tired after a day with all three kids.
>
> TIFFANY: *(calming down, and acknowledging John's point of view)* I am. But I guess you don't like falling over things after you've had a long day too.
>
> JOHN: *(giving up his need to have Tiffany say she should have made the kids clean up)* That's right. I wish that didn't happen.
>
> TIFFANY: I'm sorry if you got hurt. Let's get the kids to clean up right after dinner.

Try to Relax

In addition to the three strategies we just mentioned, being relaxed can do a lot to prevent or lessen escalating arguments. If you're in a calm frame of mind, you're much less likely to jump into anger than if you're already anxious or upset. Try these tips for feeling more relaxed and in control before discussing something important:

- Take a relaxing bath—even 10 minutes is soothing.
- Go for a walk, or just step outside for a few minutes of quiet.
- Do something restful you enjoy, such as listening to quiet music or reading.
- Take some deep breaths, followed by a cup of decaf tea or coffee.

Pattern 2: Invalidation

Invalidation is a fancy word for showing disrespect (though it's important to know that you can feel disrespected even when your partner didn't mean to do it). When partners disrespect each other in the ways we're talking about here, they put each other down. One partner says that the other person's thoughts, feelings, or character is wrong or unimportant. And that really hurts. It also can greatly damage the couple's relationship, because the person who gets put down may start to feel it's too risky to say what he or she really thinks. Avoiding a pattern of invalidation and disrespect is an important part of a happy marriage. Regularly showing contempt for each other can destroy love as fast as anything we know.

Like escalation, invalidation shows up in big and small ways. Here's an example of showing disrespect in a major way:

> RONNIE: *(shouting)* Enrique, you missed your doctor's appointment again! You can't do anything right. You're going to die young, just like your father. And I'm going to be left all alone.
>
> ENRIQUE: *(hurt)* I'm not like my father. I take care of myself.
>
> RONNIE: *(sarcastically)* Oh, right. Blowing off your doctor's appointment is really taking care of yourself. You're so stupid.

> ENRIQUE: *(very sarcastically)* And you're so smart, right? You think you know everything. But you're the one who's stupid.

It's pretty obvious that both Ronnie and Enrique are putting each other down. Neither is showing respect, and both are saying hateful, harmful things. In the following conversation, the put-downs are not as harsh, but they're still painful and invalidating.

> CHRISTIE: *(crying a little)* I didn't get that promotion today. My boss said he gave it to Sue Ellen because she has more experience.
>
> WAYNE: Hey, that's not so bad. You still have your job, right?
>
> CHRISTIE: Yeah, but I really wanted that promotion. Can't you see I'm upset?
>
> WAYNE: I see it, but you shouldn't be. It's really not a big deal.

In this example, there's no shouting and no sarcasm. And neither partner is calling the other one stupid. But Wayne is still putting Christie down by telling her she shouldn't be upset. He may think he'll cheer her up by saying the situation is no big deal, but when he tells her she shouldn't be upset he's saying that what she's feeling is wrong. If he does that often enough, Christie may decide to stop telling him how she feels. That will keep their relationship from being safe, happy, trusting, and supportive.

A third way that invalidation shows up is also subtle, but still very damaging. This kind happens when one partner tells the other something positive he or she has done, expecting to be praised for it. But the partner ignores the good work or behavior and points out a problem instead.

> STUART: *(coming home, excited and happy)* Sarah, I won the club's trail run! Look at my trophy!
>
> SARAH: Oh, Stuart, you've gotten mud all over the rug.

Being Respectful

If disrespect—either major or minor—isn't part of your relationship, three cheers for you! You're doing great, and we encourage you to keep responding to each other with love and respect. But what can you do if disrespect and invalidating arguments are part of your life? There are two important steps you can take right away:

1. Treat your partner with the same respect you'd like everyone to show you.
2. Really listen to and acknowledge your partner's words and point of view.

When you show respect and hear what your partner is saying, you're telling your partner several things. First, you're saying that your partner is entitled to his or her thoughts and feelings—even if they're not the same as yours. You're also saying that you respect your partner as a person, someone with character and worth, someone you love. You don't have to agree with everything your partner says in order to validate his or her feelings. But you do need to listen respectfully.

If you don't recognize that one or both of you is disrespecting the other until a discussion is over, there's still something you can do to prevent lasting harm. We call it the *do-over*. Just like a movie director, who thinks a scene can be handled better and calls for another take, you can call for your own second take and do your conversation over.

Here's how it works. When you realize you've blown it, that one or both of you have hurt the other, just say, "OK, let's do that over. We can talk about this in a better way." Those few, easy-to-say words can give you the chance to think about what was said, take a breath, and then discuss the point again in a kinder, more respectful way. No blame, no fault, just a way to try again.

Let's give Ronnie and Enrique the chance to do over their argument, this time respecting each other and acknowledging their partner's point of view.

> RONNIE: *(shouting)* Enrique, you missed your doctor's appointment again! *(calming down and stopping herself from disrespecting Enrique by calling him names)* I'm worried that if you don't take care of yourself you won't be here for me.
>
> ENRIQUE: *(hurt by Ronnie's anger, but acknowledging her point of view)* I guess you're afraid I might get really sick or die. I guess you really care about me.
>
> RONNIE: That's right. When you don't get your checkups, I worry about you and I worry about us.

By calming down and remembering that Enrique deserves respect, Ronnie was able to express her true feelings but not invalidate Enrique in the process. By letting Ronnie know her feelings are worthy and important, Enrique showed Ronnie that he respects her and feels her love.

Stopping an invalidating argument can be hard to do, especially when you or your spouse is really angry or frustrated. But stopping, reducing, or never getting into this negative pattern is one of the most powerful things you can do to build a great marriage and keep it strong.

Pattern 3: Negative Interpretations

When people interpret someone's words or actions negatively, they're working from the belief that those words or actions were meant to hurt them. They believe the worst instead of the best in order to confirm the bad thing they think is true. Rather than look for the positive, they make negative judgments about other people's thoughts and actions.

When partners negatively interpret each other's words or actions, handling conflict becomes much harder. That's because such interpretations create a feeling of hopelessness. It's also because, once a negative interpretation is made, it's very hard to change. Negative interpretations are also very hard to see and counteract.

Here's an example of a husband misinterpreting his wife's words because he believes she doesn't like his parents.

> MARTY: *(checking the prices of airline tickets on the Internet)* Linda, I just found some great tickets we could use to visit my parents over Christmas.
>
> LINDA: *(paying bills and worrying about their expenses)* Do you think we have the money to go this year?
>
> MARTY: *(angry)* Well, I know you've never liked them, but my family is very important to me. I'm going, even if you don't want to.
>
> LINDA: I'd be happy to go, I'm just worried about spending a lot of money right now.
>
> MARTY: *(even angrier)* Why can't you just admit that you don't like my parents?
>
> LINDA: Because it's not true. I like your parents. I'm just wondering if we need to save the money for other things.
>
> MARTY: *(storming out of the room)* Money's just an excuse. I know the real reason you don't want to go.

Do you see what happened? Linda wanted to talk about their budget, but Marty interpreted her words such that they became a slam against his parents. That's because, over the years of their marriage, Linda hasn't agreed with every one of Marty's parents' ideas. Even though Linda has forgotten those disagreements, Marty has created and held on to the belief that Linda doesn't like his parents. Marty now has a mind-set that makes him interpret Linda's words negatively whenever an issue involves his parents.

This mind-set keeps Linda and Marty from having constructive discussions. It also puts Linda at a complete loss when they talk. She can't change Marty's mind, no matter what she says. And if Marty continues to see everything negatively, in time Linda will answer him with anger and negative interpretations of her own. She may also pull away and not want to be with Marty at all.

Research shows that once you get set in a pattern of misinterpretation and thinking the worst, another negative pattern sets in. You start to feel justified in making those negative interpretations and in hurting your partner. You think it's your right to hurt your partner because you think he or she is hurting you. So you take your revenge whenever you think you've been slighted.

Fighting Back Against Negative Interpretations

We're not going to sugarcoat anything here. Seeing everything negatively is devastating to a marriage. Nor are we going to pretend that it's easy to get out of this destructive pattern. But if you work hard, you can break it. And if you and your partner always think the best rather than the worst, you can stay in this excellent pattern by continuing to give each other love, support, and respect.

There are three things you can do to control how you interpret your partner's words or behavior:

1. Ask yourself if you might be seeing some of your partner's actions in an overly negative light.
2. Force yourself to look for evidence that goes against your negative interpretations.
3. Be a relationship optimist.

When you work on this problem, dig down hard. Really think about the way you react to things your partner says. For example, if she says she's not up to going out with you to a movie, do you immediately assume she doesn't like spending time with you? Because she didn't want to go to the big party at your office a month ago? Instead of thinking the worst—that she has stopped loving you—and thinking you should say something hurtful back, stop for a second. Could it be she's just tired, because she started a new job? Maybe she'd really like to be with you—but be with you at home.

If you think you might be putting a negative spin on things, start looking hard for evidence that shows you could be wrong. For example, even if your wife didn't want to go out with you on one night, can you think of a few times she did want to be with you? Maybe last weekend she rented a video for just the two of you to watch. Or maybe a few days ago she asked if you wanted to meet her for lunch. If you find proof that she's happy spending time with you, you may be more likely to see what she says in a positive light.

Changing negative interpretations is hard. That's because you have to be less trusting of your own perceptions and more trusting of your partner's reasons for doing some of things he or she does. But putting in the work can pay off in huge ways. If you assume the best instead of the worst, you'll be much less likely to hurt your partner—and your partnership.

Let's see what could have happened if Marty had assumed the best when he talked with Linda:

MARTY: (checking the prices of airline tickets on the Internet) Linda, I just found some great tickets we could use to visit my parents over Christmas.

LINDA: (paying bills and worrying about their expenses) Do you think we have the money to go this year?

MARTY: (remembering to think the best—that Linda's concerned about money, rather than that she's looking for an excuse not to visit his parents) Well, I'd really like to see them. Do we have a lot of expenses coming up?

LINDA: Yes, we do. I guess you forgot we have that big payment due in January.

> MARTY: That's right. Well, maybe they could come here and stay with us for a few days.
>
> LINDA: I think our budget could handle that. I'd like to see them too.

By not immediately jumping to the conclusion that Linda was trying to avoid his parents, Marty was able to hear Linda's true concern. By gently responding to Marty instead of snapping back angrily, Linda kept the discussion from getting out of hand. They both listened to and respected each other. And they solved their problem as a team.

Pattern 4: Withdrawal

This destructive pattern shows up in two different ways: through *pulling back* and through *avoidance*. Both show that the person doing the withdrawing or avoiding doesn't want to be part of an important conversation. And both show that there's trouble ahead.

Why Do People Withdraw? _____

There are four main reasons why people might withdraw from conversations:

1. They're not interested in intimacy.
2. They don't want to change in some way.
3. They want to show control.
4. They don't want to get into a fight.

We don't think the first point is usually true—most men and women do want intimacy. (See the following section, "How Men and Women Deal—Differently—with Conflict," for more on this.) Points 2 and 3 are sometimes true, and they do cause damage. But point 4 is the biggest reason that partners—particularly men—pull back from discussing issues.

Withdrawal during a talk can be obvious—the person gets up and leaves the room. It can also be much less noticeable—the person just gets quieter and may finally stop talking. Someone withdrawing may also quickly agree to a suggestion. Doing this stops the conversation, even if the person has no intention of following through.

Someone who wants to avoid a conversation will try very hard to keep it from starting. This could involve changing the subject, not being available to talk, or just saying the subject isn't important enough to talk about. If, no matter what he or she does, the conversation gets going, the avoider is likely to withdraw.

Here's an example of someone refusing to talk:

LETITIA: Marcus, I really want to talk about you helping more around the house.

MARCUS: *(trying to avoid the discussion)* I can't talk about anything now. I have to leave to meet the guys.

LETITIA: *(getting annoyed)* That's just what I mean. There's a pile of dishes and tons of laundry to do, and the garbage needs to be taken out. And you're going out to play basketball. You're leaving it all for me to do.

MARCUS: *(leaving the room to look for his keys)* I can't do it now, and I can't talk about it now.

LETITIA: *(raising her voice)* You never can talk about it. But I have to have some help.

MARCUS: *(not talking, just glaring as he looks for his keys)*

LETITIA: *(even angrier)* Well, say something. We have to talk about this.

MARCUS: *(walking toward the door)* I'm not going to talk to you when you yell and act this way. I'm going to play basketball. I'll be home later.

Many couples do this ineffective, damaging dance when there are important problems to deal with. One partner pushes the issue (in this case, Letitia) and the other tries to avoid it or pull out of it (here, Marcus). The person who withdraws is usually the partner who feels more anxious about the issue. Often that person also pulls away in other areas of life—from things he or she doesn't feel confident to handle. The push–pull away situation is common—but common isn't good. Using it to handle conflict is a major predictor of unhappiness and divorce.

Changing the Dance

If neither you nor your partner withdraws from sensitive conversations, you're doing a lot to protect your partnership. You're also developing trust, which lets both of you be safely open and honest. Keep up the good work!

If withdrawal is taking place, however, it's likely to get worse. That's because the person who pushes the issue generally gets more frustrated and angry each time the withdrawer pulls away. And that makes the pursuer push harder—which makes the withdrawer withdraw more. It also leaves the issue completely unsolved.

So what can you do? Here are some ways to get and keep the conversation going constructively:

- Remember that you and your partner are a team—you're talking to find a joint solution, not to win.
- Remember that your action will cause a reaction.
- Start an important discussion gently and talk calmly—raising your voice hurts instead of helps.
- If your partner starts to withdraw, don't push the issue. Set a new time to continue the conversation. Withdrawing can be reduced when pushing is reduced.

- Talk with your partner about the fact that avoiding a problem won't make it go away.
- Look for evidence that the withdrawer cares about you—it's usually the issue, not you, that he or she is trying to avoid.

Let's take a look at how these talking tips could have helped Letitia and Marcus:

> LETITIA: *(starting the discussion gently and respectfully)* Marcus, I have something I'd like to talk about. We both work, but I do most of the housework too. I'd like to talk about sharing the housework more equally.
>
> MARCUS: *(trying to avoid the discussion)* I can't talk about that now. I have to leave to meet the guys.
>
> LETITIA: *(stopping herself from getting annoyed)* We have to talk about this some time. I need you to help me with the problem. If you can't talk about it now, what time would be better?
>
> MARCUS: *(leaving the room to look for his keys)* I don't know. Just not now.
>
> LETITIA: *(staying calm)* OK. How about tomorrow night?
>
> Marcus: *(coming back into the room and noticing that Letitia isn't pushing the issue and is respecting his wish to leave at that moment)* OK. Let's talk about it tomorrow after dinner.

HOW MEN AND WOMEN DEAL—DIFFERENTLY—WITH CONFLICT

OK. We all know it. (And we like it, too!) Men and women are different. That's no surprise to anyone. But what may be a surprise is that men and women often deal with conflict very differently.

Although it's not true in every case, men are generally more likely than women to withdraw from or avoid a potentially difficult discussion. There are several reasons why they might do this (see the box on page 35), but most often it's because they don't want to get into a fight. Men just don't seem to handle conflict in marriage as well as women do, so they shut down, thinking that by not talking they'll keep conflict from starting.

These tendencies make men and women complain about different things in their marriage. Women often are unhappy that their husbands won't open up to them, and think they don't care. Men frequently complain that their wives get upset about things too often. They feel hassled, and want more peace.

But though they often avoid important discussions because they're concerned about fights, men may actually want a difficult situation to get better. Their relationship may also be very important to them. But because they don't like conflict, it can look as if they don't care.

Women, in contrast, usually need to talk things over—openly and often. They may also need regular information about how their relationship is doing. If their husband withdraws during an important conversation about these kinds of things, they can feel shut out and that their relationship is threatened.

How Do You Think of Intimacy?

Research shows that women often believe intimacy involves verbal communication. It also shows that men most often think of intimacy in terms of shared activities. When a woman is looking for intimacy, she may want to spend time sharing feelings with her husband. A man may show his interest in intimacy by asking his wife to go on a walk or make love.

So what do they do? Again, it's not always the case, but often women will push a conversation to get the communication they need. If the husband sees the conversation as dangerous, and thinks his wife is trying to pick a fight, he may refuse to talk. And if he keeps withdrawing, his wife may push even harder.

That sets the couple squarely in Pattern 4: the cycle of pursuit and withdrawal. It also can send the couple spiraling into Pattern 3, in which one or both of them thinks the worst because of how things appear. Getting stuck in either or both of these patterns, as we've said, can be disastrous for a marriage.

Happily, our approach helps both men and women find what they're looking for. We teach couples how to have open, caring conversations (the traditional female goal) without fights or threats (the traditional male goal). Virtually all couples we've worked with have the goal of talking without fighting. This sets the stage for deep and satisfying friendship and commitment.

Handling the Differences

While we can't change the way men and women tend to handle conflict, we can change the way we deal with the differences. Several steps you can take are listed in the earlier sections "Fighting Back Against Negative Interpretations" and "Changing the Dance." Here are some other ways you can prevent the battle of the sexes.

- Accept the fact that men and women often handle conflict differently, but remember that both usually want the same things from their relationship: to be loved and to have a friend for life.
- If you're feeling that your partner's anger is the major problem in your relationship, realize that his or her anger is often a sign that there are other problems that need to be discussed. Avoid focusing on the anger; don't get angry or withdrawn. Instead, set up times to talk about the problems.
- Show respect for your partner—protecting your love means handling it with care. If you get angry easily, work on calming yourself, so that the unresolved issues underlying the anger can be discussed.
- Spend as much time as you need figuring out what intimacy means to your partner. It may mean talking about feelings to

you, but it may mean bike riding together every weekend to him. Assuming that your approaches to intimacy are the same can end up causing conflict.

- Try to connect with your partner in several ways. Couples who are the happiest share friendly talks as well as activities.
- Though you and your partner may have different approaches to handling conflict, remember that you're partners, not enemies.

⚡ POWER-UP EXERCISES

At this spot in each chapter, we're going to ask you to write a bit about what in the chapter had the greatest impact on you. It might be a pattern of behavior, a concept, a suggestion, or a point that relates to something you've seen in your own relationship. Or it might be your answer to one of the questions in the quiz. Whatever it is, write down your thoughts about it. You may want to keep a notebook or journal just for this purpose. After you've finished writing, move on to the questions that follow.

INDIVIDUAL EXERCISE

1. Think about escalation. Can you remember a recent example of it in your relationship? What is one thing you could do to keep the pattern from continuing the next time you have an argument?

2. How do you feel when your partner invalidates you? If you treat your partner disrespectfully at times, think of at least one thing you could do to stop, reduce, or avoid this negative pattern the next time you and your partner have a conflict.

3. Think of a recent time when you assumed the worst about something your partner said or did. As you think about it now, can you see another way you might interpret the situation that might be less negative?

4. Which partner in your marriage tends to withdraw the most? What do you think is the cause—fear of change, need to control, desire to prevent intimacy, or fear of conflict?

5. Which partner in your marriage tends to pursue your relationship issues? Do you think this happens because the person is worried about the relationship, wants more intimacy, or does so for a different reason?

COUPLE EXERCISE

If you and your partner have a way to talk safely and respectfully about issues, you may want to talk together about some of the issues raised in the individual exercise. If you don't feel you can talk about them calmly, you may want to wait until you've learned the necessary skills in the next several chapters. When you're confident about your ability to talk safely, come back to discuss some of these issues.

Simple Techniques for Talking Safely and Clearly

IN THE FIRST HOUR, WE SHOWED YOU HOW YOU COULD OVERCOME four negative patterns that can damage your marriage. We gave you lots of ways to break out of these patterns and keep on talking in a friendly, positive way. But it may take some time to get comfortable using the techniques in real life, or even remember to use them. We all know how easy it can be to fall back into old habits when you're in the midst of an argument. But because the negative patterns are so hurtful, we want to give you something simple you can use right now to prevent even one more ugly fight. This process will also keep you from losing your closeness as friends, teammates, and lovers.

It's called—a very fancy term—the Time Out. And it's exactly what you think it is. Just like in a ball game, when the coach calls a time out to stop the play and make a change, a PREP Time Out gives you a way to stop something negative that's happening and turn it in a new, safe direction.

TAKING A TIME OUT

In Hour 5, we're going to give you more information about the Time Out as well as other ground rules we've developed to help you and your partner talk safely, clearly, and comfortably. But here's the Time Out in a nutshell, so you can put it right in play. Just remember that a Time Out is not a withdrawal. A withdrawal takes place against one partner's wishes, while a Time Out is agreed to, to keep conflict at bay.

• Before you need to take a Time Out, decide with your partner which words you'll use to call for one. You can simply say "Time out" or "Stop" or something else that signals "We need to take a break" (it's best to think and talk in terms of "us," not "I"). Or you might want to choose something more out of the ordinary. For example, one couple we worked with used the word *hamburger* when they realized they'd gotten into an escalating argument! The word not only stopped them from hurting each other but usually got them laughing, which really cooled things down.

• Either you or your partner can call a Time Out at any time.

• Both you and your partner agree to respect either person's need for a Time Out.

• After a Time Out is called, decide together whether to drop the issue for the time being and come back to it later (we'll teach you in Hour 5 how to come back to it) or shift into a safer way of talking by using the Speaker-Listener Technique, which we describe in this hour.

You can start using the Time Out right now, whenever you need it. Even after you learn the Speaker-Listener Technique and other safe ways to handle conflict, you can still call for Time Outs. Just remember that issues don't go away if you never discuss them. So if you decide to postpone dealing with important problems, be absolutely sure to deal with them later. Set a time to follow up.

Pausing: Taking a Mini Time Out _____

If a discussion starts to escalate, or you see it's just not going well, you can take a Time Out and come back to it at another time. Or you can simply pause the conversation for one or two minutes.

Just as you would for a Time Out, either you or your partner can call for a Pause at any time. Both of you agree ahead of time to stop talking as soon as someone says "Pause." Then, after a Pause is asked for, you agree either to take a break for a few minutes and try again, or to keep talking after restarting the conversation in a calmer, more respectful way. To keep from getting back into a negative cycle after a Pause, you might want to say, "Let's forget what we both just said and start over." The key is to keep moving forward, not get stuck in the past.

COMMUNICATION FILTERS

Before we move on to teaching you our key communication strategy, the Speaker-Listener Technique, we want to spend a few minutes talking about another common communication problem, which we call "filters."

Have you ever made what you thought was a simple conversational remark to your spouse, only to have him or her jump all over you? For example, after seeing a movie you might have said, "That was really bad, wasn't it?" And your spouse answered angrily, "Then *you* should always pick the movies." You only meant that the movie didn't happen to be a good one—not that it was your spouse's fault. But for some reason your spouse heard, "You don't think I have good taste or judgment."

Things like this happen all the time, and to everyone. But this kind of miscommunication can lead to big trouble and the need to call a Time Out.

What causes words to be misunderstood are *filters*. Like a coffee filter or an air filter, a communication filter changes what passes through it in some way. This is true for both speakers and listeners. A speaker's filters, created by past experiences or present distractions, can cause the speaker to put a particular spin on what he or she tells the listener. A listener's particular filters make the listener hear something different than what the speaker said.

We all have lots of filters hanging around in our heads. They get there because of the kind of people we are: because of what we think, how we feel, what we've experienced, how we grew up. After listening to many, many couples talk, we've found five main filters that can affect the way people communicate:

1. Distractions
2. Emotions
3. Beliefs and expectations
4. Differences in style
5. Self-protection

Let's take a look at each.

Distractions

A very common filter is one you probably recognize: being distracted. Noises around you, like those from the TV or the CD player or the kids or the dog, may keep your partner from hearing what you say clearly. Internal "noises" may keep you from hearing what your partner says: you may be thinking about something that happened earlier or something you have to do later. Or one of you might be tired or on the phone, or have a hearing or speech problem that makes clear communication difficult.

Emotions

Your emotional state can have a big effect on what you hear and say. For example, being in a good mood tends to make you give a person you're talking to the benefit of the doubt. If you're in a bad mood, you tend to see and hear things negatively. Difficult feelings, such as anger, sadness, and worry, can make innocent conversations appear threatening and cause them to escalate into fights. These negative feelings may come from the here and now or still be hanging on from an earlier experience. Emotions related to a different situation can affect the way you react to your partner now.

Beliefs and Expectations

Several filters can get lodged in your head because of how you think and what you expect. For example, if you think your partner is angry with you, you're going to hear that he or she is mad at you no matter what is said. Studies show that people tend to see what they expect to see. And expectations are hard to change, because they're often based on lifelong patterns and habits. Often we don't even know expectations are affecting us until they're not met.

To add to the problem, people tend to behave in the way we expect them to behave. That's because how we think influences their behavior, as well as our own. If you expect the worst, you may get the worst. And if you put a negative spin on something, you're also likely to get a defensive answer in return. People will defend themselves when they've been misinterpreted or falsely accused. This means expectation filters can have a negative effect on both you and your partner.

Differences in Style

Every person has a unique way of communicating, based on his or her sex, culture, family background, and lots of other factors. You may be more emotional or outgoing than your partner. Or you may be more quiet and reserved. There's no right style to have. But if you and your partner have very different styles, you may have trouble understanding each other.

For example, if you were raised in a big, emotional family, where everyone shouted to be heard, you might think that speaking loudly was normal. But if your partner grew up in a calmer environment, he or she might worry or be frightened by a raised voice. This difference in style can lead to misunderstandings.

Self-Protection

This type of filter usually comes from a fear of being hurt or rejected—something we all struggle with, especially in close relationships. Fear can stop you from saying what you really feel or think—because if you don't say it, you can't possibly be hurt, right? So you protect yourself by not communicating clearly and honestly. This may not be a big problem if you and your spouse are talking about what to have for dinner or which video to rent. But if you can't talk about your fear of being fired, covering up your real feelings can make you physically and emotionally sick. And it can keep your partner from knowing what you really want and need and who you really are.

Mismatched Memories

The five filters we just discussed can cause communication problems because of couples' different backgrounds and beliefs. Another source of communication difficulty comes from a difference in couples' memories.

Memories? That's right. For example, your wife may be *sure* you told her last week that you'd fix the leak under the sink this weekend. But it's the end of the weekend, the sink is still dripping, and she's mad that you didn't do what you promised. You *know* you told her that you'd try to get around to fixing the sink if you finished several other chores. But time ran out, and you didn't get to it. Now you're mad that she's mad at you for no reason.

Who really said what? Without a tape recording of the conversation, there's just no way to be sure. But many couples get into heated arguments defending their memory—perhaps out of a need to show superiority or because they feel insecure.

Whatever the reason, "I said–You said" fights are hurtful and harmful. And they don't get you anywhere, because there's no way to determine what actually took place. Instead, you get stuck in an ongoing battle, with each of you sticking to what you remember.

How can you get out of this destructive rut? There are two things you can do to keep differences in memory from keeping you apart:

1. Don't assume that your memory is perfect. Many studies show that the human brain is no audio or video recorder, and in fact can be distorted by many influences. So there's a good chance your memory is not as great as you think it is (sorry!).
2. Don't keep arguing about something that was said in the past— even if it was said just five minutes ago. Shift over to the present, where you can say what you're feeling and thinking now.

Both of these steps may involve making one other change—in your attitude. Instead of being either defensive or aggressive, you can best approach solving a difference in memory by speaking calmly, gently, and with humility. Your instinct may be to say, loudly, "I know I didn't promise to fix the sink, and I'm not going to do it now." But you can prevent a continuing, time-wasting, destructive battle if you say, "OK. I'm not sure exactly what I said, and I'm sorry if I wasn't clear. But I want to tell you now what I meant to say."

Gentleness and humility—for solving differences in memory as well as other potentially destructive problems—are powerful tools for forging a great marriage and making your love last.

OVERCOMING YOUR FILTERS

If filters come from your background and your experiences, you may think there's not much you can do to keep them from hurting your relationship. But there are several things you can do to prevent the pain they can cause.

• Make sure you have your partner's complete attention before you say anything important—and that you're giving your full attention to him or her. Make it easy to listen to each other by eliminating all distractions. Find a quiet place to talk, and agree not to answer the phone or the doorbell if it rings.

• Don't assume your spouse is ready to talk just because you are. Ask first if it's a good time. If the answer is, "Not right now," agree on a time you'll both be willing and able to have a good conversation.

• If you know that one of your filters has kicked in, acknowledge it and let your partner know about it. For example, if you come home in a bad mood because you didn't make the sale you thought was a sure thing, tell your spouse not only what happened but also that it's put you in a bad mood. Knowing what's happening will help your partner react more gently to something angry or defensive you might say. But remember that being under the sway of a filter doesn't give you the right to treat your partner with disrespect.

• Try hard not to mind-read, or negatively interpret what your partner says because you think you know what he or she really meant. Don't assume the worst.

• Think about how your style differs from your partner's. Then talk about how those differences affect your relationship. If you recognize that you're emotional and expressive and your partner is pretty shy, it will help you to be more respectful of each other and prevent misunderstandings.

• Always discuss things gently and with humility. This will create an atmosphere of trust that should lessen fears of rejection and increase openness and understanding.

RELATIONSHIP QUIZ

Think about the filters we discussed earlier:

• Distractions
• Emotions
• Beliefs and expectations

- Differences in style
- Self-protection

Now answer the following questions about each type.

1. Does this particular filter keep you from hearing your partner's point of view? How does it happen?
2. Think of three things you can do before your next conversation with your spouse to make it more likely that this filter won't be triggered. For example, you could do something relaxing, reorganize the environment (such as by turning on the answering machine), or make a plan (such as by deciding to talk after a favorite TV show).
3. Do you think that both you and your partner have this filter? How does that make your conversations more difficult?
4. Remember some techniques you've used to keep your conversations pleasant, productive, and respectful. Do any of those techniques apply to this filter? If they do, how can you use them to handle this filter?

CREATING A SAFE AND SUPPORTIVE ENVIRONMENT

Our research and counseling experience show that there are two main times when couples have trouble communicating well: when they disagree about something, such as money, parenting, or who's supposed to do what around the house; and when they talk about sensitive issues, such as sex or loneliness. The conversation often doesn't go well because one or both of the partners is afraid that the talk won't go well, that the talk will make them frustrated, or that they'll be rejected because of something they say. Neither partner feels safe. So they may have a frustrating talk, end up in a fight, or not talk at all.

But communicating without fear is absolutely essential to a great marriage. The deepest kind of intimacy and the strongest friendships develop when partners feel safe enough to say anything and everything to each other. Research also shows that being safe at home and protected from destructive parental conflict is very important to the well-being of children.

So what can be done to help you and your partner feel comfortable enough to share feelings, ideas, and differences without fear? What will allow you to talk safely, not only to solve conflicts but to reveal your deepest desires?

First, you need to work as a team to keep the four destructive patterns we discussed on pages 22–38 from taking hold in your relationship. We've already given you a number of ways to help you do this. Second, you need to use an agreed-on, step-by-step strategy to structure your important conversations. Structure can keep discussions and emotions from racing out of control. It can also prevent frustration and chaos.

Let's go back to baseball for just a minute. There are more tips the game can give us for better ways to have a conversation. The way the game is structured gives each team a chance at bat. It says how long the game will be played. It sets the boundaries and the guidelines. If there were no structure and no rules, no one would know what to do. Every game would be chaos.

Structure makes it possible to take part in everyday activities. But it's also a powerful means for allowing clear, open, and safe communication. In PREP programs, thousands of couples have learned a highly successful, structured communication method we call the *Speaker-Listener Technique*.

USING THE SPEAKER-LISTENER TECHNIQUE

When you need to discuss something that's important or particularly sensitive, we recommend you organize your talk using the Speaker-

Listener Technique. This simple, effective approach will help you develop confidence that you can handle whatever problem comes your way—as a team, and without fear. And that will do much to put you on the path to a long and loving marriage.

If the two of you already have good ways of talking openly and safely, even when you disagree or feel vulnerable, you may not need to learn this technique. If you choose not to, be sure you both agree that you already talk well about important issues. Then use your own method of talking when the book asks you to use the Speaker-Listener Technique.

Here are the guidelines for using the technique:

Rules for the Speaker

1. Speak only for yourself. Express your thoughts, feelings, and concerns—not what you think are the Listener's concerns.

2. Use "I statements" to express yourself. For example, say, "I felt sad when you didn't show up for lunch," not "You didn't care enough about me to write down our lunch appointment." (The sentence "I think you don't care about me" might sound like an I statement, but it's definitely not. It starts with the word "I," but it expresses an opinion about the Listener, not what you feel.)

3. Don't talk on and on. Say what you need to say in small, manageable chunks. That way the Listener can take it all in. You'll have plenty of chances to say everything you want to say.

4. Stop after each statement so the Listener can paraphrase, or sum up and repeat back to you, what you just said. If the paraphrase isn't quite right, gently make your statement again in a way that helps your partner understand. For example, say something like, "That's close, but let me make it more clear." Then make your point again. This will keep the conversation moving forward and help you stay within the structure.

Rules for the Listener

1. Paraphrase what the Speaker said each time he or she stops. That means briefly repeating what you heard, in the Speaker's words or your own. If you don't understand something that was said, ask the Speaker to explain it. Then paraphrase those words. Keep doing this until the Speaker lets you know you've paraphrased the words correctly.

2. Don't argue with what the Speaker said or give your opinion about it. Only listen carefully to and repeat what the Speaker told you. Wait until it's your turn to be the Speaker to make any response of your own. When it's your turn, speak respectfully and gently.

Rules for the Speaker and the Listener

1. When the Speaker is talking, the Listener cannot talk or interrupt. To remind both of you that the Speaker always has the floor, you may want to have the Speaker hold something that represents that concept, such as a piece of carpet or linoleum. Or you can just use the TV remote or something else handy, or write "I have the floor" on a piece of paper or cardboard.

2. The Speaker and the Listener should take turns speaking and listening. The Speaker goes first, with the Listener listening. After the Speaker speaks a few times (usually two or three) and the Listener correctly paraphrases, the two switch roles (passing off whatever is used to symbolize the floor), and the Listener becomes the Speaker. Keep switching roles so that each partner has as many opportunities as needed to speak and understand. If the Speaker has a question, he or she should ask it. The Listener should then paraphrase the question to make sure it was understood. Then the Speaker should pass the floor to the Listener so that the Listener can become the Speaker and answer the question.

3. Both Speaker and Listener can call for a Pause (see the box on page 45) at any time. A Pause is especially helpful if the Listener starts giving opinions or answering back, or if the Speaker says too

much for the Listener to paraphrase. Pausing also lets you get out of a negative pattern and clear the air.

4. Focus on having a good, safe discussion, not on solving a particular problem. If you're thinking about a solution, you're less likely to really hear what your partner feels about the issue. (We'll discuss problem-solving techniques in Hour 4.)

As you use the technique, it's important that you both listen carefully and show respect for each other—even if you strongly disagree with what your partner says. That means not making a face or rolling your eyes or shaking your head or muttering under your breath. It also means waiting politely until it's your turn to speak. (Remember, you're a team, and you want this process to help.)

Paraphrasing Examples

Accurately paraphrasing what your partner says is a key part of the Speaker-Listener Technique. If you're not sure how to do it, read through these examples to get the idea.

> *Speaker's statement:* "I had a really bad day. My sister called and yelled at me for not being able to help her with her party on Tuesday. She knows I have a meeting I can't change. But she's still mad at me."
> *Listener's paraphrase:* "It sounds like you had a tough time today." Or: "Your sister's upset that you can't help her. She really let you have it."

> *Speaker's statement:* "I really get upset when you let Mara watch TV before she does all her homework."
> *Listener's paraphrase:* "You get unhappy when I tell Mara it's OK to watch a show before she finishes her homework."

> *Speaker's statement:* "I feel lonely when you spend so much of the weekend playing sports with your friends."

Listener's paraphrase: "You feel lonely because I'm out a lot on the weekends playing sports with my friends."

Paraphrasing means summing up or briefly restating what your partner told you. It's a way to tell your partner that you really heard what he or she said.

A SAMPLE SPEAKER-LISTENER DISCUSSION

Because Speaker-Listener conversations are probably an unusual way for you to talk, it may take a while to get the hang of them. Here we break down a discussion so you can see how it works.

In the example, Seth and Jane have already agreed it's a good time to talk. They've turned off the TV and turned on the answering machine. They've gotten a small piece of carpet that they'll pass back and forth to show who's the Speaker. They're remembering that they want to work together as a team, and they're planning to stay calm and respectful.

> SETH (Speaker): I've been wanting to talk about how you always answer the phone during dinner or when we're trying to have some time together. I feel very neglected when you talk with one of your friends for half an hour and leave me alone.
>
> JANE (Listener): You feel angry when I talk on the phone and not to you.
>
> SETH (Speaker): That's not quite it. I don't feel angry, I just feel bad and neglected.
>
> JANE (Listener): You feel bad when I talk on the phone with my friends when we're supposed to be spending time together.
>
> SETH (Speaker): That's right.
>
> JANE: *(now the Speaker)* I didn't know that made you feel bad.

SETH (Listener): You didn't realize I felt hurt. *(now the Speaker)* I guess I've never told you because I was worried you'd be mad at me.

JANE (Listener): You didn't tell me because you thought I'd get mad about it.

SETH (Speaker): Yes, that's right.

JANE: *(now the Speaker)* Why would you think I'd get angry?

SETH (Listener): Why do I think you'd be angry? *(now the Speaker)* Because I know you like to spend time with your friends, and I thought you'd think I was trying to keep you from them.

JANE (Listener): You thought I'd think you didn't want me to spend time with my friends.

SETH (Speaker): Yes, I was worried about that. But I want you to spend time with your friends. I'd just feel much happier if the time we plan to spend together could be just for us.

Seth and Jane are doing a great job of hearing each other. They're speaking gently and staying focused. By following the rules instead of arguing or complaining, they're keeping their talk safe, clear, and positive. They don't have to worry about being rejected or hurt.

Jane is also learning something about Seth. Without using the Speaker-Listener Technique, she might have thought that Seth just got annoyed that she was on the phone so much. But it turns out that his feelings were being hurt, and he was too worried about getting into a fight to bring it up. When you have a safe way to talk, sensitive or emotional issues are more likely to surface because they can be discussed without fear.

How the Speaker-Listener Technique Fights the Four Negative Patterns

- *Prevents escalation:* The need to stop and paraphrase after each statement makes it unlikely a conversation will get out of control.

Because the Listener has to keep paraphrasing, he or she doesn't have the chance to shout back or increase the intensity.

- *Decreases invalidation:* Paraphrasing also helps prevent disrespect. By repeating what the Speaker said, the Listener immediately shows that the Speaker was understood, even if the point isn't agreed to. The Speaker also validates the Listener by saying the paraphrase was right. It's a great way to show that the Speaker sees how hard the Listener is working to really hear what is said.

- *Stops negative interpretations:* If the Listener doesn't paraphrase correctly, the Speaker can quickly but gently let the Listener know that the interpretation wasn't right. Then the Speaker can restate what was actually meant. The process isn't meant to be a test, but is a way to make sure you're on the same page before continuing your discussion.

- *Discourages withdrawal:* This technique helps both the withdrawer and the pursuer. The withdrawer will be less likely to pull back because the structure keeps the talk safe. The pursuer is certain to be heard, so he or she won't be driven to push the withdrawer. The technique helps both partners trust that they each want a positive conversation.

DEALING WITH DOUBTS

We're completely confident that this technique can help you improve the way you communicate and thereby keep your partnership strong. Our research has proven it, and couples who take our workshops say it's one of the most valuable things they learn. But if you or your partner has any of the following objections to using it, these answers can help. Once you read through them, give the technique a try. You'll probably find that you like it.

- *It's not a normal way for people to talk.* That's true, it's not. But if your normal way of talking includes arguing and getting stuck in negative patterns, then talking in a different, "abnormal" way may be just what you need.

• *Talks go too slowly.* Yes, they do go slowly. But the slow pace lets you really hear what your partner is saying. Understanding each other is much more important than getting through the discussion fast—with no one being understood.

• *My partner never gives up the floor.* If the two of you have trouble switching from Speaker to Listener, make a rule that says you must switch roles after a certain number of Speaker statements and Listener paraphrases, perhaps three or four.

• *There are too many rules, and I hate rules.* We understand that a lot of people don't like structure, because it makes them feel confined. But the rules are there to make sure your discussions stay safe and that both partners are heard. Just like in a baseball game, the rules move the game forward and give both teams a fair chance.

• *I want to try it, but my spouse just isn't interested.* Even if your partner doesn't want to try the technique, you can still use its main ideas to improve difficult talks or keep conversations positive. One partner's use of the technique can have a strengthening effect on both partners' communication.

• *I've heard that happy couples don't naturally use this kind of active listening, so we shouldn't either.* The main reason we teach this technique is to keep couples from getting into dangerous patterns and to help those who are already engaging in destructive fighting to get out of danger by talking safely about important issues. Our research shows that happy couples are less likely to engage in these patterns, which means they don't have the same need to use the Speaker-Listener technique as do unhappy couples. One key to marital happiness is having the skills and the confidence to handle your differences and talk about sensitive issues without fighting in negative ways. Our research shows that using the Speaker-Listener Technique when you are having trouble communicating is one way to protect and preserve your love.

TIPS FOR USING THE TECHNIQUE

Once you're ready to start using the technique, follow these hints for making it as successful as possible:

• For one week, use the technique to talk about things that aren't important or sensitive. (See the Power-Up Exercises that follow for suggestions on subjects you might discuss.)

• Practice the technique for 15 minutes at a time several times a week.

• Don't try to solve problems. Just try to have a good discussion in which you learn and acknowledge each other's point of view.

• After three successful discussions, choose a topic that you slightly disagree about. If an argument develops, stop talking and choose a safer topic. Discuss the first topic again after you've had several more successful practices. Work up to using the technique for discussing more difficult or sensitive issues.

• Remember to practice respecting each other every time you practice the technique.

⚡ POWER-UP EXERCISES

INDIVIDUAL EXERCISE

As usual, start this section by thinking and writing about what in this hour had the greatest effect on you. Then go on to the following exercise.

COUPLE EXERCISE

If you and your partner are interested in trying the Speaker-Listener Technique together, the following can help you get started. If you're working on this program on your own, see page 14 for some helpful suggestions.

Start by talking about something that's not too difficult and that's not likely to make you argue. If you're not sure what to talk about, try one of these topics:

• What would be your dream vacation?
• What would be your dream job?

- What would you do or buy if you had an extra $500 to spend on something fun?
- What makes your favorite movie so great?
- Why is _____ someone you look up to?

As you discuss your topic, each of you should take several turns being the Speaker and the Listener. Remember to use the skills you learned.

If the Listener starts talking about his or her own feelings or information (this might show up as a "Yes, but . . ." sentence), or if the Listener asks a leading question or starts to direct the conversation, then please stop. The Listener should remember that he or she will have plenty of time to say things when participating as the Speaker. Be sure the Speaker thinks the Listener is repeating back what the Speaker actually said.

Remember that the goal is not to solve a problem but to hold a discussion in which the Listener really hears and paraphrases what the Speaker said. Try not to offer suggestions for fixing a problem but instead talk about your feelings, needs, and concerns. And remember that the more the two of you practice the technique, the easier and more comfortable it will be to use. That, in turn, will help you have successful conversations when you discuss more difficult issues.

Handling Your Issues

WHAT WOULD YOU SAY MOST COUPLES FIGHT ABOUT? When we ask couples in our workshops, the top two answers are usually issues about money and issues about children. Research shows that other big issues have to do with sex, communication, in-laws, leisure activities, alcohol and drugs, religion, careers, and housework, with different issues popping up at different stages of a relationship. Although these particular issues may not cause conflict in your relationship, all couples have difficult issues to deal with.

Issues alone, though, don't always cause fights. Issues often erupt into arguments when they're set off by what we call *events*. Events are the everyday happenings we all experience, such as going to work or watching a movie. They're what make up our lives. But events that revolve around difficult issues can spark those issues into explosive fires.

For example, if a couple's major issue is money, any event involving money can trigger an argument. This could be writing a check to pay a bill or giving the children their allowances. If one or both partners is concerned about money, the smallest, most innocent act involving money can result in a potentially damaging fight.

We all have issues, and we all experience events. So you may be wondering if it's possible to keep events from turning your issues into arguments. This hour will show you that it is. You're going to learn how to deal with triggering events and how to handle your issues—those that are easily seen and those that are hidden—so that your marriage stays safe and strong.

DEALING WITH ISSUES BEFORE THEY GET WORSE

Even though we all have issues, few of us discuss them when things are going well. If an issue seems to be under control and not causing any trouble, we tend to let it be—until an event throws it front and center and triggers a fight. Instead of dealing with a problem when we're calm, cool, and collected, we end up dealing with it under the worst possible circumstances.

Take Dylan and Lisa. A few days ago their son Scott came home from an activity later than they'd agreed. Dylan and Lisa never discussed the issue, and went on to other things. Now Scott has come home late again. When Dylan gets home from work after a long day, this is what happens:

> DYLAN: *(tired from work, and expecting a warm welcome)* Hi, Lisa, I'm home.
>
> LISA: *(yelling angrily from the kitchen)* Dinner is going to be late because Scott came home late again and didn't help me.
>
> DYLAN: *(annoyed at the unpleasant greeting, but not wanting to get into a fight)* Well, we'll just eat later then. I'm sure he didn't mean to be late.
>
> LISA: *(still angry)* If you'd set a better example, maybe he'd be on time.

This wasn't the welcome Dylan expected, to say the least. And it probably wasn't the way Lisa thought the evening would go, either. The problem is, Lisa and Dylan have a history of disagreeing on parenting issues, and because their disagreements often lead to fights, they generally don't discuss them. (The main issue here is parenting, but there's also a hidden issue—Lisa's concern that Dylan's lateness is setting a bad example for their son. We address hidden issues on page 72 of this hour.) When Scott was late the first time, they didn't discuss what to do about it. Now he's late again, and that event has triggered a fight that was waiting to happen.

Instead of addressing the problem when they had time and were relatively calm, now Lisa and Dylan are facing it under very trying circumstances. Dinner has to be made. Everyone's tired. Expectations aren't being met. Angry words are being exchanged.

Lisa and Dylan are like most of us. They don't sit down to talk about major issues on a regular basis because it's so hard to deal with differences and conflicts. Instead, they end up having to handle the explosive events that result from their lack of communication. And that continuing turmoil can be a real drag on their marriage.

It also can make couples feel as if they're walking on eggshells. They know there's a problem, but they don't want to discuss it. They also know it's bound to resurface, and that makes them anxious. Will they get into a fight tonight? Will things fall apart when their parents are visiting this weekend? When will the next crisis erupt? This kind of worry and anxiety can wear away the good things in any marriage and keep partners from feeling safe and loved.

If you know you and your partner have a particular issue that needs to be worked out, try to talk about it when things are calm and crisis free. Setting aside regular times to talk can ensure quiet, constructive conversations. Even when things are going well, the two of you need to deal with important issues before they become continuing concerns.

You can use the Speaker-Listener Technique (see Hour 2) to help you through the process if you find that talking naturally doesn't work.

Just be sure to give yourselves plenty of time to talk, and remember to be respectful and loving and really listen to each other's point of view. If you handle your issues as teammates, in a positive, constructive way, you'll be able to control your issues instead of letting them control you.

Here's a summary of how to handle issues before they catch fire:

- Set aside regular times to work on them.
- Talk when things are calm and you won't be interrupted.
- Talk without fighting, using the Speaker-Listener Technique if needed.
- Face your issues as a team, with respect, love, and humility.

Controlling Negative Emotions

Part of managing issues involves managing negative emotions. That means not letting anger, sadness, hostility, or other potentially destructive emotions become automatic reactions to conflict. By controlling your negative emotions, you can hear what your partner is saying and respond constructively and lovingly. It's important to manage your negative emotions when either you or your partner is upset.

We find that men often have a harder time managing their negative emotions when their wives are upset than when they themselves are upset. That's because husbands often believe that their wife's anger is the problem, not the issue itself. But that isn't the case. The wife's anger isn't the problem. No, it's the issue that's the problem, it's the issue that provokes the anger. And it's the issue that needs to be dealt with.

Anger, however, can be harmful to a relationship if it's hostile and disrespectful. So the most helpful thing men can do is help their wives calm down so that they can hear what their wives are saying. On the same point, women need to remember that their husbands are more likely to listen to what they're saying if they can express their concerns clearly and gently.

To take control of your negative emotions during a discussion,

- Explore ways to soothe yourself when you start to get upset. Stop negative interpretations or thoughts that fuel anger. Try taking a few deep breaths, a Time Out, or a Pause (see pages 44 and 45).
- Remind yourself that withdrawing or letting your negative emotions rule will not solve the problem.
- Speak gently and calmly.
- Treat your spouse with respect.

KEEPING EVENTS FROM STARTING A FIGHT

As we said earlier, the best way to stop issues from erupting at inconvenient times is to talk about them before they're triggered by events. We encourage you to pinpoint your major issues now and set aside specific times to work on them. Being proactive is a great way to keep your team together and create an environment that's happy and satisfying.

Sometimes, though, despite our best intentions, events can send us straight toward an argument. If the issue has been buried, the smallest thing can catapult it to the surface. A word, a letter, even a look can release the beast. All of a sudden you're on the edge of a damaging fight.

Then what can you do? Happily, there's a lot.

Let Annoying Events Bounce Off You

The key to keeping events from turning issues into arguments is to remember that you're in charge. You don't have to let events provoke you. You can decide, together or individually, that whatever has happened isn't important enough to fight over. For example, if your partner says something that pushes your issue buttons, you can choose to simply let it go.

You probably do this often when you're at work or with friends—you don't allow a quick conversation or a brief action to jeopardize your job or your friendship. Well, you can do the same thing in your marriage by being positive instead of negative and by letting annoying or provocative events just bounce away. Try to remember that you and your partner are in this thing together and that you don't want a word or an action to jeopardize your future.

Controlling Negative Self-Talk

In addition to keeping events from controlling you, you also need to keep your own negative thoughts at bay. Negative "self-talk" can be caused by annoying events. For example, suppose you have been out at an evening business event and expected to come home to a clean kitchen. But the dirty dishes and pots and pans are everywhere. "Here we go again. He never helps out when I need him to" may be what jumps into your mind. But this kind of response can increase your anger and cause you to act in less than loving ways. In fact, studies show that negative self-talk is one of the primary causes of nasty conflict.

You can control your negative interpretations by thinking the best instead of the worst. Listen to explanations and look for evidence that goes against your negative ideas. (For more on controlling negative interpretations, see pages 33–35).

Choose Another Time to Talk About the Issue

Although you don't want an event to push you into a big argument, you should still remember that the issue it brings up is probably important. That means it has to be discussed—but it doesn't have to be discussed now. To prevent an argument, you can say, "I know this issue is a problem. But this isn't a good time to deal with it. Let's decide on a time to talk about it later." When you say this to your partner, make sure you also hear it yourself. Telling yourself something constructive will help you avoid making a negative interpretation and keep anger away.

Postponing a discussion doesn't mean that something important didn't just happen or that you're not upset about the underlying issue.

It just means that you want to discuss the problem when you're both more able to handle it well.

Learn from These Examples

Our research has shown that disagreements involving in-laws are often the cause of arguments, especially for engaged couples. Even if your in-laws are perfect (despite the jokes, we know there are some great ones out there), it can be difficult to adjust to new relationships and family dynamics. Let's see how one couple with in-law issues let an event trigger an argument that not only ruined their evening but also hurt their marriage. Then we'll see how they could have avoided this situation.

Kendra and Marshall have been married just a year. Kendra has been concerned because she feels that her mother-in-law intrudes on their life. Marshall's mother calls him all the time, drops in on the two of them at home, and arranges get-togethers without checking with Kendra. But Kendra has been afraid to discuss the problem because she's afraid Marshall might side with his mother.

Now Kendra and Marshall were on their way to see a movie—the first time they'd been out together in some time. But just as they pulled away from their apartment, Marshall's cell phone rang. It was his mother. And he talked with her nearly the whole way to the movie theater.

KENDRA: *(very annoyed)* You know, this is the first chance we've had to go out together in a long time. And just now you let your mother take up half our evening.

MARSHALL: *(getting annoyed too)* It wasn't half our evening. And she needed to talk to me.

KENDRA: *(even angrier)* Couldn't it have waited until tomorrow? She's always interfering, and you always let her get her way.

> MARSHALL: *(very angry now)* She doesn't always interfere.
> You've just never liked her.

The rest of the evening didn't go well go for Kendra and Marshall. They had set out to have some fun, but a phone call triggered an issue that hadn't been dealt with because of mutual fear and avoidance. Instead of having an evening to build their love and friendship, they ended up exchanging angry words.

How could this have been prevented? Kendra could have brought up her concern long before. Then she and Marshall could have been working on the issue as a team. They could have set aside time to talk over solutions when they were both calm and free of distractions.

If Kendra and Marshall had addressed the problem earlier, two things could have happened when Marshall's mother phoned. Marshall would have understood that the phone call was going to take away time from Kendra, and that would hurt both her and their marriage. So he could have said, "Mom, I'd love to talk to you, but this isn't a good time. I'll call you first thing tomorrow morning." If Marshall had talked to his mother anyway, Kendra could have chosen to postpone bringing up her concern. She might have thought, "Great, there he goes again, choosing his mother over me. But I really want to have some fun tonight and spend time together. I'm going to let this go for now, and set a time to talk about it another day."

Instead of arguing, their conversation after the phone call could have gone like this:

> KENDRA: *(remembering to speak calmly)* It really annoys me
> that you took that call from your mother.
>
> MARSHALL: *(annoyed)* What should I have done, hang up on
> her?

KENDRA: *(taking a deep breath so she won't react with anger)* You know how we've talked about your mother's involvement in our lives. There's definitely more to talk about, and I want to do it soon. But we wanted to have fun tonight. So let's talk about this another time.

MARSHALL: *(respecting Kendra's wishes and speaking with humility)* That's a good idea. I'm sorry I took the call, and we can talk about it tomorrow. But let's have a good time now.

Kendra could have vented her anger. And Marshall could have defended his position. But none of that would have solved the problem—it probably would have made things worse. By speaking calmly, preventing negative emotions, and choosing to talk about the problem at a better time, Kendra and Marshall were able to separate the issue from the event. They not only made it possible to have fun together that night but also strengthened their marriage for the long term.

Three Ways to Talk

Through our workshops and counseling experiences, we've come to believe that couples engage in only three kinds of talks. Although all three are part of married life, it's the third that's most important.

1. *Casual talk:* This is the kind of talk that's needed to deal with the nitty-gritty of life: Who's going to shop for groceries? What time will you be home from work? This kind of talking should be polite, respectful, and upbeat.
2. *Conflict talk:* This type of talking is for dealing with the inevitable differences and disagreements. Conflict talk should take place only when both partners are ready. It should be respectful and safe, with no fighting and with lots of trust. Many of the techniques in the first part of this book focus on helping partners successfully negotiate conflict talks.

3. *Friendship talk:* This kind of talking builds intimacy and strengthens connections. It's talking about the things that matter and that you share and enjoy. Friendship talking can be as simple as sharing what's going on or what's important to you. It's also listening carefully and supporting your mate when he or she is feeling vulnerable. Friendship talking is the kind of talking couples do when they're falling in love, and it should continue throughout their relationship. Without friendship talks, you may forget what brought you together and why you want to stay that way.

Couples who are safe at home engage in conflict talk only at appropriate times and safely, perhaps using a structured technique like our Speaker-Listener Technique. The rest of the time they enjoy talking together as partners and as friends.

UNDERSTANDING HIDDEN ISSUES

Most of the time it's very clear which issues are triggered by events. They have to do with everyday things, like money, household chores, or children's homework. But sometimes fights break out around things you can't put your finger on. Or you start out talking about one subject and suddenly find yourselves discussing something completely different.

Remember Dylan and Lisa? They started arguing because their son was coming home later than he was told to. A parenting issue seemed to be at the root of their fight. But when the argument escalated, another issue became clear. Lisa was also angry that Dylan was coming home late and setting a bad example for their son. A parenting issue was definitely involved. But there was also a deeper, hidden issue: Lisa's concern that Dylan wasn't doing his part for their family.

Kendra and Marshall seemed to have a hidden issue too. Kendra was annoyed that Marshall let his mother interfere. But deep down she worried that he cared more about his mother than he did about her.

Hidden issues are unexpressed expectations, needs, feelings, and fears. And they're often the cause of the most frustrating and destructive arguments couples have. Because they're buried so far down, they can have frightening energy when they break through the surface.

Hidden issues generally are associated with six relationship areas: power and control, caring, recognition, integrity, commitment, and acceptance.

Power and Control Issues

Whenever the two of you need to make decisions, power issues can develop. Who will take out the garbage? How much money should go into savings? Which movie should we see? Does the baby need a better day-care center? The decisions can be big or small. But when your partner questions your status or level of control, a power struggle can result. If it seems like one partner's needs are always more important than the other's, power and control issues may be affecting your relationship.

Caring Issues

Hidden issues about caring relate to how much one partner feels cared for and loved by the other. If one partner feels the other isn't meeting his or her emotional needs, hidden issues can surface. For example, your husband might think you should have a snack waiting for him when he gets home from work. You may think that's something he can take care of himself. But if your husband's mother always put snacks out for him before your marriage, he may feel that if you don't do it too, you don't love him enough. You may be arguing about who should prepare food, but the deeper concern is really a unique issue about caring.

Recognition Issues

Issues about recognition stem from how valued you feel. If you think your partner doesn't appreciate the things you do or what you've accomplished, you may feel undervalued, or even ignored. Many men don't feel that their wives value the work they do to provide for their families. Many women say their husbands don't appreciate all the work they do at home, whether or not they work outside the home as well. If partners feel unappreciated, they may push hard to get the recognition they need. This drive for appreciation can be the cause of many arguments.

Integrity Issues

Integrity issues are similar to caring issues, but instead of being about how much you or your partner cares, these issues have to do with your motives, values, or standards. If your partner questions your integrity, you can feel judged, insulted, and disrespected. For example, if you forgot to pick up groceries on the way home and your spouse says it's really because you're inconsiderate, you can feel as though your character has been attacked. This can make you feel defensive and cause you to make negative interpretations of your own. Then both you and your partner may end up feeling hurt and invalidated.

Commitment Issues

Will we stay together—no matter what? That question is at the heart of most commitment issues. When you're certain that your love will last, you feel safe and trusting. But if you worry that your partner might leave, it can affect many of your interactions. For example, one couple we worked with seemed to be having a money problem. They had separate checking accounts, and the husband was very unhappy about it. Each time a bank statement arrived, the partners had a fight. It turned out that the wife had wanted a separate account to buy special things, such as presents for her husband. But the husband thought it was because she wasn't really committed to the marriage and that having her own account would make it easier for her to leave him. Because the husband never mentioned this worry, it provoked an argument when each monthly statement appeared.

Acceptance Issues

Everyone wants to be accepted. It's a universal desire. So most people try to find acceptance and avoid rejection wherever they can. This strongly felt need and equally strong fear are at the root of many arguments, and can be triggered by almost any event.

The need for acceptance also drives all the other issues—power, caring, recognition, commitment, and integrity. Hidden underneath those issues is the worry that your partner doesn't accept who you are. For example, James, an engaged man we worked with, always took a one-week fishing trip each year with several of his friends. His fiancée Michele wanted him to promise that he wouldn't take these trips once they were married. But James wanted to continue, as a way to keep up important relationships with old buddies. Michele said that meant he preferred his friends to her. James said not going would be giving up control and would make him feel as though she thought he wouldn't be a good husband. Although issues of caring, control, and integrity were involved, at the root of them all was an acceptance issue. Both James and Michele were concerned that their partner didn't accept them for who they are.

RELATIONSHIP QUIZ

Take this quiz to see how events and issues may be affecting your relationship.

1. Identify three events that regularly trigger conflict between you and your partner. For example, going out to dinner might trigger a fight about how much money you should be saving.
2. Taking deep breaths can help control negative emotions. Think of two other things you can do to keep negative emotions from spilling out and that will help you calm

down when you're too upset to talk or be with your
partner productively.

3. Think about how you and your partner talk most of the
   time. How are your conversations split among friendship
   talk, conflict talk, and casual talk? What do you think the
   ideal division would be?

4. Think about the six types of hidden issues: power and
   control, caring, recognition, integrity, commitment, and
   acceptance. Then answer the following questions about
   each:

   • Does this issue reflect concerns you have about your
     relationship?

   • Have you had this concern in other relationships?

   • When did this issue start for you? For example, you
     might have experienced it through your parents'
     relationship.

RECOGNIZING HIDDEN ISSUES

Because hidden issues are just that—hidden—it can be hard to know if
you have any. The following four signs can help you identify hidden
issues so that you can keep them from hurting your relationship.

Wheel Spinning

Have you ever thought, "Here we go again" when you and your spouse
started discussing something? That's a good sign that you have a hidden issue. No matter how often you talk about the problem, you
never get anywhere. That's because the problem you're talking about
is not the real issue—the real issue is hidden. When you keep discussing a problem that never gets solved, you can end up feeling hopeless and helpless.

Small Events Triggering Big Arguments

When an apparently unimportant action sets off a huge fight, you can be pretty sure a hidden issue is at work. Remember the couple whose bank statements provoked problems? The arrival of a piece of mail sparked a major explosion because of a hidden commitment issue.

Avoidance

If you or your partner keeps avoiding a certain topic, it's likely that a hidden issue is involved. For example, you and your spouse may practice different religions but never talk about it. You may both be worried that your partner won't love you if he or she knows what you really believe. Or you may never talk about sex because one or both of you fears being rejected for your ideas. This kind of avoidance often reflects an acceptance issue, and can put your marriage at risk.

Scorekeeping

If you're feeling neglected or hurt, you might start keeping score when you think you're being mistreated. You might think, "He disrespected me four times this week." "She only did the dishes once, and I did them five times." Scorekeeping generally means that a hidden issue is in play—often a recognition issue or an issue of control. Whatever the issue is, it's not being talked about. Instead, you're keeping track of when you feel wronged. This means that you're working against each other rather than as a team.

WORKING ON HIDDEN ISSUES

As you've been reading about hidden issues, have you recognized any that affect you? If you've thought hard and not identified any, congratulations! You've been sharing your deepest thoughts and keeping differences or concerns from becoming buried problems.

If you've found that one or more hidden issues are affecting your relationship, there's a lot you can do to prevent them from damaging your love.

- As soon as you recognize that an issue exists, agree to talk about it, either now or at a specific later time.
- When you're ready to talk, you can use the Speaker-Listener Technique to allow an open, positive, caring conversation. Or you can choose to talk in a different way that you know is safe and respectful.
- Remember our baseball theory and think and work together as a team.
- Don't try to solve the problem. Instead, concentrate on hearing each other's thoughts about what's going on. Often hidden issues can't be solved if they're part of your personality or history. But you can still focus on understanding the issues together.
- Respect your partner and consider his or her feelings. By accepting and acknowledging what your partner says, you'll be building intimacy and creating trust.
- Call a Time Out (see page 44) if the discussion starts to escalate or if you think it's not going well.
- Establish regular times to talk about issues so they don't keep getting worse.

What We Can't Change

Hidden issues develop from the kind of person you are. They can result from your worldview, a good or bad experience, or the way you were treated in the past. Because those things are so much a part of you, it can be hard to solve the problems they cause.

But to solve your problems, it's not necessary to completely change who you are or try to become someone you're not. It is possible to have a very happy and successful marriage even though you and your partner disagree about some things. The secret is tolerance, compromise, and a willingness to let both of you be the people you are.

If you understand each other's issues, you can soothe them or make them less damaging. You can also learn to accept and understand each other better. And that, in turn, will help you develop trust and intimacy, and deepen your love.

Using the Speaker-Listener Technique

Remember the engaged couple James and Michele? Michele didn't want James to continue going on fishing trips with his friends once he and Michele were married. But James wanted to remain close to his friends. The acceptance issue they face could lead to big problems in their marriage. But by using the Speaker-Listener Technique, they can bring the issue into the open and not let it hurt their marriage. They can also learn more about each other and increase the likelihood of a happy future.

Here's how their Speaker-Listener talk might go:

> MICHELE (Speaker): *(holding a piece of tile to show she has the floor)* James, I really don't understand why you want to keep going on those fishing trips. Once we're married, we should spend all our free time together.
>
> JAMES (Listener): You're saying that you don't understand why I would still want to go fishing with my friends after we get married.
>
> MICHELE (Speaker): That's right. I feel hurt that you'd rather be with your friends than with me. *(She hands James the piece of tile.)*
>
> JAMES (Speaker): I'm sorry that your feelings were hurt. I love you, and I want to spend a lot of time with you. But my friends are really important to me too. I'd like you to respect that.
>
> MICHELE (Listener): You really do love me and like to spend time with me. But you want me to respect your wish to stay close with your friends too.

> JAMES (Speaker): You've got it. I want you to understand that I love you, but I also want you to understand that my friends mean a lot to me too.

During their talk, James and Michele stayed calm and respectful. They took the time to really hear what their partner was saying. By taking advantage of the safety and structure provided by the Speaker-Listener Technique, they were able to soothe a sensitive acceptance issue that might have hurt their marriage.

Hidden issues can cause a lot of conflict. But when you're able to discuss them openly, they can actually help you and your spouse become closer and more loving.

⚡ POWER-UP EXERCISES

INDIVIDUAL EXERCISE

Start this section by thinking and writing about what in this hour had the greatest effect on you. Then go on to the following exercise.

COUPLE EXERCISE

Bringing hidden issues into the open can make them less likely to hurt your marriage. But discussing hidden issues can arouse strong feelings. To help you learn how to deal with issues safely, try discussing hidden issues using the Speaker-Listener Technique.

Before you start, take another look at James and Michele's conversation above. You can also review everything about the technique on pages 52–55. When you start to discuss your topic, remember to be sensitive and respectful. Take turns being the Speaker and the Listener, and make sure the Listener always paraphrases the Speaker's words correctly. If you have trouble at any point, Pause, or agree to start over using a more constructive approach. Or call a Time Out and try again later.

Be sure to set a time limit for your talk. You can do a lot in 15 or 20 minutes and feel good about what you accomplished. That's much better than talking for an hour and risking falling into old, negative habits.

When you're ready to start, one of you should take the floor and talk about a hidden issue that's part of your relationship. When you continue the discussion later—most hidden issues require several conversations to become clear—the other partner can start. You may want to schedule a second discussion as soon as you finish the first.

Solving Your Problems

IN THE FIRST THREE HOURS OF THIS PROGRAM, we talked a lot about the typical, normal kinds of conflict even the happiest couples might have. All partners have differences, and all have problems. But although you may have turned to this book for help in eliminating those problems, or to learn how to handle everyday problems well in order to prevent more serious ones from developing, so far we haven't talked about how to *solve* any of them.

Well, there's a reason: our research and real-world experience have shown that couples seem to reach better solutions if they first discuss their issue respectfully and understand each other's point of view, even if they don't agree. Understanding and accepting each other's perspective not only is more important for maintaining and enhancing your connection than solving most problems but also builds the foundation for good solutions.

In the three hours you've put in so far, you've learned many techniques you can use to hold safe, positive, caring conversations about your issues. We've also touched on ways to strengthen your connection and protect your love, which we'll expand on in later hours. Now that you've learned about and practiced those important approaches, it's time to learn the techniques for problem solving.

Ready? Let's go.

FOUR POINTS ABOUT PROBLEM SOLVING

The PREP approach to solving problems is based on four important points:

1. All couples have problems.
2. Couples who are most effective at solving problems work on them as a team. (But that doesn't mean you can't work on solving problems on your own if your partner isn't doing his or her part right now.)
3. Most couples hurry to solve their problems, which doesn't give them time to address concerns, especially hidden ones. Those concerns can resurface, so quick fixes don't last.
4. Not every problem can or needs to be solved. Sometimes accepting and appreciating differences are what's necessary.

Let's take a look at each idea.

All Couples Have Problems

As we've said, problems do occur, even in the happiest of marriages. Couples may have different problems, but no relationship is problem free. Problems can change as partners move through life—for example, issues about child rearing may taper off when children leave for college. But some problems may stay much the same throughout a couple's partnership. For example, if you're extremely neat and your spouse is more on the messy side, issues about housekeeping may continue for years. (You may be very aware of this already!)

Studies have also shown that couples tend to argue about certain things depending on where they are in the development of their relationship. Engaged couples often have problems with jealousy and future in-laws. This reflects their need to establish boundaries with other people. During the first year of marriage, many couples report having difficulties with communication and sexual issues, reflecting their increased interaction. Later, most frequent issues are about money and child rearing, and smaller concerns focus on chores, time together, in-laws, jealousy, alcohol, and drugs. When couples become empty-nesters, arguments often revolve around communication, conflict, and sex. Couples in second marriages say child rearing is a major concern. And for almost all couples, no matter where they are in their relationship, money is often a big source of conflict.

Whatever your problems, or whatever problems may come later, rest assured that you're not the only ones who have them. And rest assured that the problem-solving perspective and tools in this chapter can help you accept and love each other despite your differences.

Who Wants to Solve the Problems?

Women are generally the ones who bring up current problems. But that doesn't mean their goal is always to have their spouse tell them how to solve them. Wives often tell us they want their husbands to listen to them, not necessarily to fix their problems. Many women find value in talking about issues openly.

Most men, though, typically would rather do something active than talk. They tend to want to solve problems, quickly and simply, and feel helpless and even withdraw when they think they can't.

Instead of plunging in to try to fix things, both men and women should first listen to each other's concerns, calmly and constructively. The way you begin communicating about a problem is crucial to being able to eventually solve it together, or deciding to accept and value the differences between you. In fact, many couples tell us that the need to solve a problem sometimes disappears after a good talk.

Teams Solve Problems Best

When a problem comes up, do you and your partner face it together? Or do you deal with it separately, in different ways? In many marriages, partners approach problems as contests that only one of them can win. They get locked into a cycle of trying to conquer each other instead of the problem. But just as in baseball, working as a team gives you the best chance of handling your challenges.

Let's take a look at a problem faced by newlyweds Mario and Sylvia. Like many couples, they both work outside the home. And like many couples, they argue over who should do the housework. Because they don't face the problem as a team, their arguments generally go like this:

> SYLVIA: Mario, the house is really a mess. We've got to do something about keeping it cleaner.
>
> MARIO: *(annoyed, and trying to watch TV)* I know it's a mess. But I want to relax when I get home. Housework should be your job.
>
> SYLVIA: *(angry)* Why should it be my job? I'm just as tired as you are when I come home from work. And I'm a lot neater. You don't even pick up after yourself.
>
> MARIO: *(angry now too)* I'd do more around the house if you made as much money as I do.
>
> SYLVIA: *(very hurt and upset)* Well, that's really nice. I might not make as much, but I work just as hard. I'm not going to do all the housework too. You have to do your share.
>
> MARIO: Well, I'm not going to give up my free time. And I'm not going to talk about it either. *(He gets up and storms out of the room.)*

What went wrong here? A lot of things. To begin with, Sylvia brought up the problem at a less than ideal time. Both she and Mario were tired after a long day at work. And Mario was watching TV. Then both of them disrespected each other by pointing fingers and placing blame. Instead of working together, they tried to put the problem on their partner. Finally, after Sylvia kept pushing the issue, Mario refused to deal with it by walking away. They were both angry and upset for hours.

Now let's assume that Mario and Sylvia have invested a few hours in reading this book and learned more about problem solving and how important teamwork can be. They realize that chores are an issue for them, so they decide on a quiet time to talk about it. Now, instead of fighting and hurting their marriage—and still having a messy house— their conversation goes like this:

> SYLVIA: Mario, the house is really a mess. I'd like to talk about what we can do to keep it cleaner.
>
> MARIO: I'd like it to be cleaner too. But I make more money than you, so I think housework should be your job.
>
> SYLVIA: That's so unfair. My job may not pay as much as yours, but I work really hard too.
>
> MARIO: *(getting tense and tempted to lash out, but taking a deep breath and trying to stay constructive)* Yeah, you do work hard. I guess I wasn't thinking that you'd be just as tired as I am, and not want to clean up either. But I feel so overworked already that I don't think I can do any more.
>
> SYLVIA: You know, I really don't want you to have to do more, I just need to do less somehow. Can we take one small step together now? Why don't we both put away the stuff in this room? Then at least one room will be clean, and it'll go fast if we do it together.
>
> MARIO: OK. Then we can relax the rest of the night and talk some more over the weekend about how to keep things from piling up again.

Isn't this a much better outcome? Mario and Sylvia treated each other with respect, really listened to each other's concerns, and worked on their problem together. Instead of staying angry for hours, each partner took a few moments to work on staying calm and preventing the discussion from escalating. They put just a small amount of time into talking without fighting. No one lost, and neither did their marriage.

By sharing ideas and feelings and working as team, Mario and Sylvia protected their love and began to solve their problem. Couples often tell us they don't have the time to use the skills we teach, but Mario and Sylvia are evidence that you don't have to waste hours and hours being angry and distant.

Quick Fixes Don't Last

All too often, we rush to solve a problem. The problem is unpleasant, so we try to get rid of it as fast as we can. The theory is, if we fix everything now, we can avoid conflict and get right back to enjoying ourselves.

The problem with this theory is that it usually doesn't work. When a problem is "fixed" too quickly, the two of you can miss an underlying issue. And that important issue can come back to haunt you, usually in the form of more problems and more conflict.

Two key factors generally rush couples to find solutions: time pressure and the urge to avoid conflict.

Time Pressure

Most of us live in a "now" environment. Everything needs to be done right away, so we don't take the time to really look into things carefully. But when you respond without having all the information, you can make a bad choice or act inappropriately.

Thinking you have to solve a problem quickly can push you into making a poor decision. That's not terrible if you're just deciding whether to go out for pizza or for hamburgers. But if you're trying to figure out which school is right for your child or whether you can afford a new car, taking the time to understand all the issues will help you make a good, long-term choice.

Conflict Avoidance

Often couples rush to solve their problems because the thought of arguing over them is just too scary. An issue comes up and they decide quickly on a solution. Whew. No worries. No fights. But then the same issue comes up again, and again. Soon someone gets upset, and the argument the two have been trying to avoid erupts anyway.

Most people don't enjoy arguing. But by trying to avoid a fight, you can miss an opportunity to discover what's really the problem. And if you don't know what the problem is, there's no way you can solve it permanently.

Not Every Problem Can Be Solved

Many people don't want to believe that some problems can't be solved. The whole concept goes against our Western "can do" way of life. It also can affect couples' feelings about their marriage: if their problems can't be solved, there must be something wrong with their marriage.

Thinking this way is not a good way to go, because believing something is seriously wrong can make you think you should divorce. To protect your happiness, you'll want to do the best you can to solve your problems. But it's very important to understand that you may not be able to solve every problem that comes your way, and that even the happiest couples have issues they've lived with for the whole length of their marriage.

For example, Russell and Jan both smoked for many years. Finally Jan was able to quit, but Russell didn't want to. Though they'd had a great marriage, their new situation began to cause conflict. Jan pushed Russell to quit. Russell got angry and defensive. Arguments sprang up constantly.

After talking and working with Jan and Russell on their problem, we became convinced that nothing was going to solve it, at least right then. Russell was going to keep smoking and Jan wasn't. But they loved each other and wanted to stay together. To help them do that, we showed them how to protect all the things that were good in their marriage. In a way, they built a fence around the problem and agreed on how to keep the problem from ruining the great things in the marriage.

Working as a team, they figured out where and when it would be OK for Russell to smoke in the house, what to do when they went out, and other issues that revolved around smoking. The major issue couldn't be solved. But Russell and Jan were able to continue enjoying a loving, satisfying marriage.

That's a key point to remember. Even if some of your problems can't be solved, you can still have a great, lasting marriage. Listening to each other and understanding each other are more important for keeping a strong connection than finding a solution to every problem. And for many problems, understanding each other is the only solution you need.

That's so important that we want to repeat it. Some things can't be changed. Some problems won't be solved. But none of that matters very much if you accept, understand, and have compassion for each other, and keep your priorities straight. You *can* live with differences. Nobody is perfect. Not even the best relationship is conflict free. What counts is devotion, respect, and commitment, which we'll tell you more about in later hours.

RELATIONSHIP QUIZ

Before you can solve problems, it's important to know just what they are. The following quiz was developed in 1971 by researcher David Knox and has been used in our work for many years. The quiz helps you and your partner understand the areas that are giving you trouble and how much trouble each issue is.

Please rate each of the following areas on a scale of 0 to 100. If there's no problem with an area, rate it 0; if it's a severe problem, you might rate it 90 or 100. Be sure to rate all areas. Use separate pieces of paper to complete the quiz, then compare your ratings with your partner.

_____ Money	_____ Recreation
_____ Jealousy	_____ Communication
_____ Friends	_____ Careers
_____ In-laws	_____ Alcohol or drugs
_____ Sex	_____ Children or parenting
_____ Religion	_____ Household chores
_____ Time together	_____ Other

THE PREP STEPS TO PROBLEM SOLVING

When you're dealing with issues that are hard to handle, studies show that it helps to take a structured approach. As you've seen, the structured Speaker-Listener Technique is great for discussing important issues. Taking turns as Speaker and Listener and following the other guidelines allow you and your partner to talk safely and confidently.

When it comes to solving problems, structure helps again. The PREP approach to solving problems is structured and straightforward. There are only a few steps, but each is very powerful. They help you solve issues as a team. They also let you see issues more clearly and keep conflict away.

Before we get into each step, we want you (and your partner if your partner is reading this book with you) to agree to do three things:

1. Be willing to work (together) to solve your issues.
2. Be creative, flexible, and willing to experiment with change.
3. Practice all the steps, even if you generally don't like structure.

Agreeing to these suggestions will help you get the most out of the process. And practicing the steps will help you build confidence that you can deal with almost any problem that comes your way. Once you learn the technique, you can decide later if you want to use each specific guideline.

Here are the steps for handling problems:

1. Discuss the problem
2. Solve the problem
   a. Set an agenda
   b. Brainstorm
   c. Agree on a solution
   d. Follow up

Discuss the Problem

Our work has shown that it's much easier to solve a problem if you and your partner do so in an atmosphere of respect and acceptance. To create that atmosphere, it's best to talk first about the issue for a while before trying to solve it. By talking first, you lay the foundation for finding a solution.

Whether the problem is big or small, set aside a specific time to talk about it. Then keep talking until you both understand it. Be sure that both of you also feel understood by your partner, even if you disagree. For example, you might understand that your partner feels sad about a problem the two of you are having while still having a different take on the issue. A good way to reach understanding is to use the Speaker-Listener Technique (you can review the technique on pages 52–55). The structure of the approach lets both of you be heard. It also lets you handle sensitive issues without fear or anxiety.

Be Clear About Your Concern

As you talk, be sure to give your partner clear, specific information. The real issue can be missed if you don't express exactly what you mean. For example, if you're upset that your wife drank too much at a party, you might say, "You really made a fool of yourself last night." But if you're actually concerned that she might be an alcoholic, it would be much better to say, "When you drink a lot at parties, I get embarrassed at things you say, and I get worried you have a drinking problem." A specific message like that has a better chance of being heard than the first more general, angry, disrespectful statement. It also expresses the deeper worry about alcohol abuse, as well as the lesser concern about behavior at a party.

In their book *A Couple's Guide to Communication,* Gottman, Notarius, Gonso, and Markman discuss a great way to help you make clear, accurate points. They call it the *X-Y-Z statement.* An X-Y-Z statement goes like this:

"When you do X in situation Y, I feel Z."

Here's an example: "When you track mud into the kitchen (X) after working in the yard (Y), I feel really annoyed (Z)." Another example is "When you tell your friends something (X) I wanted only you to know (Y), I feel like I can't trust you to be discreet (Z)." The X-Y-Z statement is a positive alternative to the way people often make complaints: "You're such a slob," "You did it again, you jerk," and the like.

When you're trying to solve a problem, it's easy to start blaming each other. It's also easy to make general statements that don't really say what you mean. This can be frustrating and can cause the discussion to escalate. Although no one really likes to hear complaints, X-Y-Z statements let you identify a problem clearly and calmly and tell your partner how you feel about it. X-Y-Z statements are particularly powerful for changing annoying behavior and counteracting negative interpretations.

Why are these statements so successful? It's because of the Z. When you focus on talking about your feelings instead of blaming your partner for the problems, your partner can relax and be more able to listen well. And that's the key to good communication.

Solve the Problem

After a really excellent discussion, you may discover that you no longer have a problem to solve. By talking about a problem, you both can learn what's been happening and get your feelings out in the open. It may turn out that you don't need a solution as much as you needed to air the issue. Our experience has been that 70 percent of the issues couples face just need to be discussed rather than solved. We've also seen that partners don't need answers as much as they need to feel listened to and loved.

Having a great discussion may be all you need to do. But in many cases a problem does still need a solution, so follow the next steps to find the answer. The discussion you had will make the problem solving go more smoothly.

1. Set an Agenda

The first step to solving a problem is to set an agenda for working on it. This means making very clear exactly what you're trying to solve. It also means determining in what order you'll work on each part of the problem and when you'll do the work.

Say that your issue is money. You had a very good discussion about all the areas involved. Now you want to set up a process for solving the various problems.

Start by writing down all the things you talked about in the discussion period: credit card debt, how to save more, who will pay the bills and balance the checkbook, how to make a realistic budget. Now put all the issues in the order you want to work on them, so that you handle just one thing at a time. It's a good idea to choose the easiest thing to work on first. In this example, it might be deciding who will pay the bills. Something more complex, like planning a budget, can be dealt with later, after you've had some practice with problem solving. (For more on money issues you can also refer to the Resources and Training section at the end of this book.)

Once you've determined the priorities, set a time to work on each issue. For example, you might choose every Wednesday night at 8:00 until you've covered all the topics.

If your issue has only one part, agenda setting is much simpler. First, make it very clear exactly what the issue is. For example, your problem may be whether or not you should let your teenager go to a party on Saturday. Since there's only one question, you don't need to decide what you'll talk about first. Just choose a time to work on the problem when you're both relaxed and ready.

If a problem seems too huge to be solved, don't worry. Just break it into parts and take it one small part at a time. (Remember our baseball theory? Every game is played just one pitch at a time.) Decide what needs to be done first, then what next. By doing your best and being patient, the chances are very good that you'll find a workable, satisfying solution.

2. Brainstorm

To come up with a great solution, it helps to have lots of possibilities to choose from. Brainstorming can provide you with plenty of suggestions and stretch you to think in new ways.

As you brainstorm, keep these guidelines in mind:

- Write down each idea as it's generated.
- Accept and consider every idea, even if it sounds completely crazy.
- Try to make all suggestions positive. Problem solving is about what you can do, not what you can't or won't.
- Don't criticize or make comments about each other's suggestions (that means no eye rolling or making faces, either).
- Be creative—say whatever comes to mind.
- Have fun with the process—a sense of humor will help.
- Keep going until you have as many suggestions as possible.

Loosening up and letting the ideas flow will give you a good supply of solutions to choose from. But remember that brainstorming can take time. If you jump on the first thing that sounds good, you may miss out on a better solution one of you may think of later.

3. Agree on a Solution

Now is the time to go over all the ideas you generated and choose the best one. The goal here is to decide on a specific solution you both agree to try. If one of the suggestions is the obvious choice, agreement should be simple. But if each of you prefers a different answer, a compromise is in order.

Compromise means that one or both of you may need to give up something you want. Hmmm, you may be thinking. I don't like the sound of that. But compromising doesn't mean losing. Even though you give up something, you actually win. That's because you put the needs of your relationship above your own. And that helps protect your love and keep your marriage strong. It's more likely you'll have a great marriage if you don't always insist on getting your own way. In fact, many couples end up preferring a different solution or a combination of solutions they brainstormed together rather than the solution each originally wanted.

As you discuss each possible solution, look at both the pros and the cons. Keep in mind that the best solution is something that's doable and agreeable to you both. When you make your choice, summarize the solution so you both understand it. You may even want to write it down.

4. Follow Up

Agreeing on a solution and putting it into place are two key parts of solving a problem. Another important part is following up to see if the solution is working. If you don't follow up, it may not be clear that the two of you chose the right answer. And if you didn't choose the right answer, a problem can continue or return, sometimes worse than before.

When you choose a solution, plan a specific time to see how well it's working. A week is usually about right, but two or three weeks may be better for some issues. If you find that the solution eliminated your problem, there's nothing else you need to do—except be happy.

If the problem still continues, you may want to adjust the solution a bit to see if that works it out. For example, you might decide that you're going to take turns doing the dishes, but your turn keeps coming up on nights you have late meetings. Then you would agree to adjust the schedule and check soon to see if it's working. If it's not doing the trick, go back to the list of solutions you came up with and try something else. Then check on the progress of this solution in another week.

Following up may not seem that important once you've agreed on a solution. But knowing you'll follow up will encourage you to give the solution your all.

A PROBLEM-SOLVING EXAMPLE

Now that you've learned about the PREP problem-solving process, we want to show you how it actually works. The following example walks you through one couple's efforts to solve an important issue. We've broken the process into the separate steps so that you can see how each contributes to finding a workable solution.

In the example, Derrick and Yvonne have a two-part problem. The big issue is money, but part of it is high credit card debt, and part of it is the fact that Yvonne plans to quit her job to stay home with their new baby. Derrick and Yvonne have recognized they have a problem and set aside a quiet time to work on it. They plan to use the Speaker-Listener Technique for their discussion.

Discussing the Problem

YVONNE: *(acting as the Speaker, holding the floor)* I'm really glad we're talking about this. I'm very worried about our money situation.

DERRICK (Listener): You're worried about money. But I'm not sure what it is about money that's worrying you.

YVONNE: *(still the Speaker, and trying to make it more clear what worries her)* I'm worried that our credit card bill is always so high. And I'm wondering if maybe I shouldn't quit my job after our baby is born, because we'll have so much less money.

DERRICK (Listener): You're worried because our credit card bill is high. You're also worried that maybe you shouldn't quit your job because we'll have less money to live on, especially when we have the baby.

YVONNE (Speaker): That's right. I want to talk about how we can spend less and if it's OK for me not to work for a while.

DERRICK (Listener): You want to talk about ways to spend less and whether or not it's OK for you to stay home with the baby for a while.

YVONNE (Speaker): Right. I know we have a lot of things we need, but we seem to spend so much. If I stay home with the baby we'll have a lot less. But I also think staying home is the right thing to do. I want to give the baby a really good start.

DERRICK (Listener): We need to buy a lot, and if you quit your job we'll have less money. But it's important to you to give the baby a good start, and that means being home.

YVONNE (Speaker): That's what I think. Tell me what you think.

DERRICK: *(taking the floor and becoming the Speaker)* I've been worried about this too. I don't want to get into a lot of debt the way my parents did. That was awful. But I also think you should stay at home with the baby, at least for a while.

YVONNE (Listener): You're worried about money too. You're afraid we'll get into debt the way your parents did. But you think it's good for the baby and me to be at home, at least at first.

DERRICK (Speaker): Yes. Do you think we could spend less? I looked at the last credit card bill, and it looks like you bought a lot of things.

YVONNE (Listener): *(getting defensive)* I did buy a lot of things, to get ready for the baby. *(remembering not to escalate the dis-*

cussion and only to paraphrase what the Speaker says) I mean, you wonder if we could spend less, and you think I bought a lot last month. Can I have the floor now if I paraphrased you right?

DERRICK (Speaker): OK. You paraphrased me right. Here's the floor. *(He gives Yvonne the floor.)*

YVONNE (Speaker): When you say it looks like I bought a lot of things, it makes me feel like you think I'm the only one who spends a lot.

DERRICK (Listener): You think I'm saying you're the only one who spends a lot. If that's right, can I have the floor again?

YVONNE (Speaker): That's right. Here's the floor. *(She gives Derrick the floor.)*

DERRICK (Speaker): I'm sorry it sounded like I thought you're the only one who does a lot of spending. Actually, I don't think that way. I do a lot of spending too, I just didn't do much last month.

YVONNE (Listener): You don't think I'm the only one who spends a lot. I'm glad to hear that.

DERRICK (Speaker): Yeah, we both do our fair share of spending. So if you don't work for a while, I wonder if there's a way for both of us to spend less for a while. What do you think? *(He hands Yvonne the floor.)*

YVONNE (Speaker): I think there is a way. But first, do we agree that I should stay home with the baby? It's very important to me.

DERRICK (Listener): You think there's a way to spend less. But first you want to know if I agree that you should stay home with the baby.

YVONNE (Speaker): That's right. Do you think I should? *(She gives Derrick the floor.)*

DERRICK (Speaker): I think you should. My mom was able to stay home with my brother, but she couldn't with me. I always felt like I missed out on a lot.

YVONNE (Listener): You agree I should stay home with the baby. You wish your mother could have stayed home with you.

DERRICK (Speaker): Right. So it looks like we agree on that. That's good. Let's set a time to figure out some ways to spend less so that we won't feel squeezed when you quit your job.

Solving the Problem

Now that Derrick and Yvonne have thoroughly discussed their problem, they're ready to solve it. At this point, they stop using the Speaker-Listener Technique but continue to talk calmly and respectfully.

1. Setting an Agenda

DERRICK: OK, we know we need to talk about ways to spend less money. It seems like that has two parts: stuff we have to buy all the time, like groceries and things for the baby. And then things we spend on every now and then, like taking a vacation or getting something big for the house. Can you think of anything else?

YVONNE: Well, I think that's it for where we spend money. But besides saving money, I'm wondering if we shouldn't talk about ways to make more too. We decided I should take a leave from my job to stay home with the baby. But maybe I could do some freelance work from home. Or maybe every now and then you could work some overtime.

DERRICK: That's a good idea. Let's write this stuff down. Our big thing is saving money. We need to talk about saving money on everyday things and on bigger things. We also should talk about maybe making some extra money while you're at home with the baby. So which do you think we should talk about first?

YVONNE: I think we should look at ways we can save first. That will probably make us feel less worried about my not having a paycheck soon. Once we figure that out, we can start to think about ways to bring in some extra money.

DERRICK: Good, I agree. I think talking about ways to save is probably going to take a couple of hours. When do you want to talk?

YVONNE: This Monday night is good. I can get home early from work that day. What about you?

DERRICK: That's good for me too. If we need more time, we could talk on Thursday too.

YVONNE: That sounds good. So on Monday night we're going to brainstorm ways to spend less. Let's set the next Monday night for working on ways to bring in some more money.

DERRICK: OK, I'll write it on the calendar.

2. Brainstorming

YVONNE: Let's get started. I have one idea. A new discount store just opened. I could try shopping there for the last few baby things we need.

DERRICK: Good idea. Here, I'm going to write down everything we come up with. I was also thinking maybe we could find other couples with new babies, so that when we want to go out we can trade baby-sitting. That should save a lot.

YVONNE: Great. I could also ask my sister if she'd ever baby-sit.

DERRICK: I'll add that to the list.

YVONNE: For the bigger stuff, how about if we plan on just a few day trips to the lake this summer, instead of going away for a week? Since the baby will be so little, it will be hard to travel far anyway. If we don't have motels to pay for, we'll spend a lot less, but we'll still be able to get away.

DERRICK: Good. How about stuff around the house? I know we've been planning on getting a new dryer, because the one we've got doesn't hold much and there's going to be a lot more laundry to do when the baby comes. But maybe we could hold off on that for a while.

YVONNE: I'd rather think of another way to cut expenses. That dryer is pretty old, and if we use it night and day to keep up with the baby's stuff, it's not going to last much longer anyway.

DERRICK: I guess that makes sense. I won't put that on the list. How about if I start doing our car tune-ups again? I used to do them, and they're no big deal.

YVONNE: That's a great idea, if you think you'll have the time. Let's put that on the list and see if it works out. As far as bringing in some extra money, I could see if my boss would let me do some contract work from home. And I could ask some of our friends if they'd like me to do their bookkeeping too.

DERRICK: That's good. I'll ask my boss about doing overtime. We can talk about some more ideas for bringing in extra money when we meet next Monday. Right now let's think of some other ways to save. *(They continue brainstorming until they have a list of 10 possibilities.)*

3. Agreeing on a Solution

DERRICK: We've got a good list here. I like your idea of trying to shop at discount stores when we can. And I really like the idea of trying to meet other couples with young babies. We could save money by trading sitting. We might also be able to trade things like clothes and toys later on, to save some more money.

YVONNE: I like that too. It would also give us more friends to do things with. What about asking my sister to baby-sit?

DERRICK: I'd like to hold off on that for now. She might want to have us sit for her kids in return, and they're pretty wild right now.

YVONNE: That's true. Let's try to meet some new people first. There might be a new-parents group at church. Or maybe you could talk to people at work to see if they might want to start an exchange group with us.

DERRICK: Great. What about saving on the bigger things, like vacations?

YVONNE: How about if we look into some fun places we could go with the baby that aren't far away?

DERRICK: I can check with people at work. And maybe your sister will have some ideas. Let's work on all of those things for three weeks: shopping at discount stores, meeting new people with kids, and checking out some inexpensive vacation ideas. Then let's see how we're doing. Once we've got a good start on saving, we can brainstorm some ideas for bringing in more money while you're home.

4. Following Up

After three weeks, Yvonne and Derrick met to see how their plan was going. They were happy to find out that the shopping they'd done in two discount stores was helping them spend less. They also had joined a group for new parents at their church, and it looked promising. In addition, Derrick had talked to several people at his office about starting a group to help each other out with baby equipment and baby-sitting.

Derrick and Yvonne's plan for finding fun, inexpensive places for getaways didn't go as well. They had asked several friends at work for ideas, but hadn't heard of anything interesting. They decided they would ask Yvonne's sister and also go online to search for good local places.

In addition to continuing to work on getaway ideas, Derrick and Yvonne went through the problem-solving process again, this time to work on more ways to budget more carefully. They figured out what their spending limit should be each month after Yvonne took a leave of absence, and decided to write down every purchase they made to keep track. They also decided to meet once a month to see if they were keeping to their plan. In addition, they set up a schedule to work on ideas for generating more income.

PROBLEM-SOLVING TIPS

To help the process help you the most, follow these suggestions:

• If you get bogged down, it may mean you're not working on the problem as a team. Try harder to be respectful, generous, and open to your partner's ideas.

• Getting bogged down can also indicate that an important part of the issue wasn't discussed completely. Take a Time Out and go back for more discussion. You can do this as often as you need to so that you're able to work together without negative feelings getting in the way.

• Depending on your problem, the process can take a short or a long time. If your problem has several parts, it may take a while to solve them all. It may also take several sessions to agree on one solution. Try not to get frustrated when it seems you're not reaching conclusions. Working on a solution will eventually get you there.

• If your problem seems to have no solution no matter how hard you work on it, you can still use the process to strengthen your marriage. Follow the steps to find ways to protect the great things in your partnership from the problems generated by the unsolvable issue. Doing that will put you in a much better position than if you let the unsolvable problem define your relationship. It will also help you accept each other more fully, differences and all. (See page 89 for more on handling an unsolvable problem.)

⋙ POWER-UP EXERCISES

INDIVIDUAL EXERCISE

Start this section by thinking and writing about what in this hour had the greatest effect on you.

Next, turn the following negative statements that couples often make to each other into X-Y-Z statements. Follow the formula "When you do X in situation Y, I feel Z." We've handled the first two as examples. You do the rest.

Negative statement: You never listen to me.

X-Y-Z statement: When you won't turn the TV off after I say I'd like to talk to you about something, I feel hurt and resentful.

Negative statement: You're such a slob.

X-Y-Z statement: When you leave your dirty clothes on the bed instead of putting them in the hamper, I feel angry and taken advantage of.

Now you try some:

You're never affectionate with me.

You always want to do things your way.

I always have to tell you everything 10 times.

You never pay attention to me.

Bonus exercise: X-Y-Z statements are also great for recognizing positive behavior. Think of three things your partner does for you and write X-Y-Z statements for them. Then share them with your partner.

COUPLE EXERCISE

Now that you've got the idea of how the problem-solving process works, try using it to solve a problem of your own. Choose a problem that's not too serious and that's not likely to cause conflict. For example, you could work on the problem of what you should do for fun this weekend. Or you could choose one of the least severe issues you marked on the quiz on pages 90–91.

As you work on the problem, follow these suggestions:

- Set aside about 30 minutes to practice problem solving uninterrupted.
- Follow the model: discuss the problem, set an agenda, brainstorm, agree on a solution, set a time to follow up.
- Check back with the appropriate parts of this hour if you need support as you go along.
- Practice the process a few times a week for several weeks to gain skill and confidence for handling tougher issues.

HOUR 5

Great Ground Rules for a Great Relationship

IN THE PREVIOUS HOURS YOU'VE LEARNED PROVEN STRATEGIES for talking safely, handling important issues, and solving problems. These strategies will help you enormously as you team up to handle both the predictable and the unpredictable issues you'll face as the two of you grow as individuals and as your relationship develops over time.

Another great way to manage the conflict in your life is to agree to a set of ground rules. Ground rules? In baseball, ground rules establish things like whether or not a ball is considered in play when it hits the top of a particular fence in a particular stadium and bounces back onto the field. Ground rules establish what's fair and what's not. And all teams follow them.

Ground rules also apply to marriage. The six we've developed will help you handle the big issues in your marriage as well as the everyday, smaller ones. They'll set the guidelines for you to handle disagreements fairly, respectfully, and calmly as well as keep both you and your partner on safe, level ground. Because you agree to the rules ahead of time, they're already in place when conflict occurs. By sticking to them you'll be able to keep your discussions from getting out of control and to express yourselves without fear.

The ground rules that follow are the six we've established for our workshop couples. They were designed to do two things: minimize conflict and provide a way for couples to deal with difficult matters. We think these rules will be great for your relationship. In fact, they may be so helpful that you'll want to stick them on the fridge or keep them in a handy spot so you can refer to them whenever you need to.

Ready to take the field? Play ball!

Ground Rule 1: When conflict escalates, we'll call a Time Out or a Pause. Then we'll try talking again with the Speaker-Listener Technique. Or we'll agree to talk at a specific later time using the Speaker-Listener Technique.

Ground Rule 1 was actually discussed in Hour 2 (see pages 44–45) because it's so important that we wanted you to learn it right away. In fact, you may have already followed this rule during Speaker-Listener Technique practices or during a real disagreement. It's an excellent way for you and your partner to stop the negative patterns of escalation, invalidation, withdrawal, and negative interpretations (see pages 22–38 if you want to brush up on the danger signs).

Just to remind you, here again are the main points to remember about the Time Out and the Pause:

Time Out
- Before you need to take a Time Out, decide with your partner which words you'll use to call for one.
- Either you or your partner can call a Time Out at any time.
- Both you and your partner agree to respect either person's need for a Time Out.

- After a Time Out is called, decide together whether to drop the issue and come back to it later, or shift into a safer way of talking.

Pause
- If a discussion starts to escalate, or you see it's just not going well, you can pause the conversation for one or two minutes.
- Just as you would for a Time Out, either you or your partner can call for a Pause at any time. Both of you agree ahead of time to stop talking as soon as someone says "Pause." Then, after a Pause is asked for, you agree either to take a break for a few minutes and try again, or to keep talking after restarting the conversation in a calmer, more respectful way.

Using Time Outs and Pauses

Researchers have discovered that couples who don't have ways to stop damaging fights don't do well over time. Happier couples have ways to signal each other when they need to calm down or keep conflict in check. The Time Out and the Pause are two effective ways to handle conflict well. They let you and your partner calm down as well as change the direction of a conversation that's gone off track.

Agreeing to and following Ground Rule 1 will do a lot to keep things cool. But if your partner tends to call a lot of Time Outs, he or she may be using it to withdraw. If that seems to be the case, you may need to remind your spouse that he or she agreed to a firm time to discuss the problem again. Then you need to make sure that the discussion takes place.

If things were really heated when a Time Out or Pause was called, you may not be able to resume talking in just a few minutes or even in a few hours. You may not even be able to set a time to come back to the discussion at all. That's OK. You can wait to set a time to talk after things have calmed down. (To customize this rule, you may want to agree that you won't wait more than a certain amount of time, perhaps 24 to 48 hours.)

But what if your partner refuses to talk about the issue at a later date? Unless your relationship is physically dangerous, the best thing to do is keep trying. Do your best to talk with your partner about the issue, but without hostility. This may mean some added conflict in the short term, but that may be better than just dropping an important issue. It will likely help to use some of the suggestions we give later in this hour about how to raise concerns in the most constructive ways. You want to keep important issues from being buried, only to have them resurface at a bad time.

Managing Your Behavior and Your Emotions

Taking a Time Out will help keep an argument from escalating. But if you and your partner don't eliminate the angry thoughts and feelings that caused the need for a Time Out in the first place, they'll still be with you when you talk again. Calming your emotions and relaxing your body will help you resume talking with respect, humility, and an open mind.

Try these suggestions to relax your body and control your emotions:

- Take several long, deep breaths.
- Lie down with your eyes closed and think positive thoughts.
- Do something relaxing: go for a walk, read, play with your pet or your kids—whatever you enjoy. Do it for at least 20 minutes.
- Remind yourself that anger will hurt both your marriage and your health. Repeat to yourself, "My anger is under control."
- Watch out for negative interpretations. Making negative judgments about your partner's motives can increase your anger and stress your body. You can calm yourself by giving your partner the benefit of the doubt.
- Follow the suggestions you came up with in the box on pages 66–67 that asked you to think of ways to calm your negative emotions.

Ground Rule 2: When we begin to have trouble communicating, we'll start to use the Speaker-Listener Technique.

When the going gets tough, it's important to have a structured, safe way to talk. That's the Speaker-Listener Technique. We showed you in Hour 2 how the technique works. We've also asked you to practice using it during several not-too-sensitive discussions. Now we want you to agree to put the technique into play whenever you begin to have trouble communicating.

Whether or not one of you calls for a Time Out or a Pause, you can always switch from a regular conversation to a Speaker-Listener conversation. Sometimes you don't need to stop a conversation as much as you need to make sure that it will continue safely, lovingly, and effectively. Agreeing to use the Speaker-Listener Technique when either of you feels it will be helpful means that you both want to handle a difficult issue in a positive, caring way.

Besides using the technique to prevent escalating fights, you can also customize the rule to use it before a conversation gets into trouble. For example, you may know that you often get into escalating arguments when you talk about sex. Now you have a concern about sex, but you don't want to get into a major battle. To have a safe, positive conversation, you could say, "Honey, I'm really worried about our sex life. I want to set a time to talk about it using the floor." Saying this will let your partner know that the issue is important. And the Speaker-Listener Technique will let you talk about it safely and really hear what each other has to say.

Ground Rule 3: We will separate discussing problems from solving problems.

We've seen in our work that couples can't solve problems permanently and well until both partners understand both the issue and their partner's ideas about it. We've also found that separating problem solving from problem discussion keeps couples from rushing into premature solutions. Too often partners want to agree on a solution just so the problem will go away. But that can lead to making poor choices.

Whenever you have an issue to work on, be sure to discuss it thoroughly first. Don't even think about trying to solve it at that point. When you think you've covered everything, answer these questions:

- Do I really understand my partner's point of view?
- Do I really think my partner understands my point of view?

If either of you answers no to either of these questions, you're not yet ready to move on to problem solving. Talk some more until both of you feel comfortable going to the next step.

Some couples who are very comfortable using the Speaker-Listener Technique and very experienced working on issues customize this rule to allow problem solving to directly follow problem discussion. But if you're less experienced, take a good break between the two.

Ground Rule 4: Either partner can bring up an issue at any time. But if one partner doesn't want to talk about it, he or she can say, "This is not a good time." That partner then takes responsibility for setting a time to talk in the near future.

This ground rule has a very specific purpose: to make sure that you don't have important discussions when one or both of you isn't ready to talk. If this ground rule isn't in place, partners can bring up difficult issues at the worst times. For example, you may want to talk about a jealousy issue, and you're feeling calm and prepared. But your wife may be trying to get the baby to fall asleep. She may be tired, grumpy, and distracted—not the best state to be in for a sensitive discussion. If she doesn't want to talk right then, you might get upset and think she doesn't care. But this ground rule can prevent that from happening. It can also prevent a damaging talk.

Ground Rule 4 assumes two important points:

1. Both you and your partner know when you're capable of discussing something with all the attention it needs.
2. You both respect each other's right to say, "I can't deal with this right now."

Saying you can't deal with something now may sound like avoidance to your partner. But the second part of the ground rule takes care of that possibility. Whoever postpones a discussion is responsible for setting a new time to talk. Agreeing to that point ensures that although a discussion has been delayed, it will eventually take place. When you agree to the ground rule, it's a good idea to agree to a postponement time limit. That could be no more than 24 to 48 hours, but you can adjust the time to suit you both.

One way you might want to customize this ground rule is to agree on some times that are never good for bringing up important issues. For example, one couple we worked with agreed that neither of them would ask to hold a significant talk within 30 minutes of their usual bedtime. They decided that relaxing at that time was much more important and that they would be much too tired to give an important issue the attention it deserved.

Ground Rule 5: We will hold weekly couple meetings.

Most people have very busy lives. If you and your partner do, you probably find it hard to set aside time to deal with problems or things that are important to you. But holding weekly meetings is a great way to show that nurturing your marriage is a high priority. It also gives you a specific time to discuss issues if no other time is available.

Just 30 minutes of couple time each week can do great things for your partnership. You can talk about specific problems if you have any. Or you can talk about your relationship or about activities that are coming up. Just about anything that involves the two of you can be discussed during your weekly meetings.

One big advantage of having regular couple times is that it can reduce much of the day-to-day pressure on your relationship. Say, for example, that you have a complaint about something. But you can't find a time that you and your partner can talk about it soon. Just knowing that your weekly meeting isn't far off can keep you from griping about your issue and pushing your partner to talk about it. You can relax, and so can your spouse.

Our work with couples has shown that it's best to set up a specific time limit for your meetings. Thirty minutes is a good length, but you can agree beforehand to lengthen or shorten the meeting to meet specific needs. Or you can customize this rule by agreeing to have more than one short meeting a week. Just keep your meetings short enough that they don't become hard to get through.

It's also a good idea to know ahead of time the kind of talk you'll be having (see pages 71–72 for a review of the three kinds of couple talk). If you're going to discuss a problem, the meeting will be a time for conflict talk. For these meetings it's helpful to use the Speaker-Listener Technique. If you're going to talk about your relationship or about things that are happening that week, you'll be using friendship or casual talk, in which the Speaker-Listener Technique isn't needed. Just remember that meetings are a time for some kind of talk, not a "date time" in which you listen to music or do something else together.

Once you start holding regular couple meetings, you'll probably find that your confidence increases and your communication skills improve. Conflict will probably lessen too. In fact, things may go so well that you might decide you don't need to hold any more meetings.

That would be a mistake. If you stop, you're likely to find that things were going so well in good part because of the meetings. When you stop setting aside time to talk, conflict can creep back in and uncertainty can return. We encourage you to continue having meetings even when things are going great. If you want, you can cut back to just a few meetings a month rather than one every week.

Ground Rule 6: We will make time for the great things in marriage: fun, friendship, and sensuality. We agree to protect these things from conflict and from discussions of difficult issues.

Ground Rule 5 encourages you to set aside time each week to talk about important issues in your relationship. Ground Rule 6 asks you also to set aside time (as much as works for you) for all the fun stuff in your marriage—the things that brought you together in the first place.

By now you know that conflict is inevitable and that it's important to handle your problems well. But it's also extremely important to spend time together that's not devoted to your issues. Happy, satisfied couples make time to have fun together, talk as friends, make love, and relax—time when differences aren't discussed and problems are off-limits. These protected times nurture your relationship because they let you just "be," without worry, conflict, or fear. (There's lots more about the importance of friendship, fun, and sex in Parts Two and Four of this book.)

How often you enjoy issue-free time together will depend on your schedules. But we want you to agree to set aside at least some time each week to do nothing but have fun—just the two of you. If an issue comes up during this time, call a Pause or a Time Out. Then agree to postpone the talk until your next couple meeting. If necessary, use the Speaker-Listener Technique to refocus on the real reason you're together right then: to have a good time and enjoy each other's company.

RELATIONSHIP QUIZ

Answer the following questions to identify the need for ground rules in your relationship. Several no answers indicate you would benefit from the structure they provide.

1. Do you keep yourself from falling into the destructive behavior patterns (escalation, invalidation, negative interpretations, and withdrawal) described in Hour 1? Does your partner?

2. Do you have ways to break these patterns when they get started? Does your partner?

3. Do you have a way to talk safely and respectfully with your partner about difficult or emotional issues?

4. Do you and your partner always talk about issues as a result of events, or do you set aside specific time to address your concerns?

5. Do you and your partner talk about a concern until you both feel heard and understood? Or do you try to fix a problem right away and only talk about things when the "fix" doesn't work?

6. Do you and your partner talk about issues at times when you're not trying to have fun and share physical or emotional intimacy?

GRIPING CONSTRUCTIVELY

The goal of our six ground rules is to establish an environment that allows partners to handle conflict well. Part of handling conflict well is making sure that you express concerns in a positive way.

That's not easy. Probably all of us have gotten angry during an important discussion and said negative things we later wished we hadn't. But it's important to remember that negative communication in any form can damage your relationship. So we want you to try a better way to let out your strong feelings: griping constructively. In fact it's probably a good idea to think of griping constructively as a kind of honorary seventh ground rule.

But how do you gripe about something constructively? Doesn't griping mean you tell your partner you don't agree or that you're upset about something? And doesn't that mean you're being negative?

Actually, it doesn't. It means you're expressing your opinion or your feelings. The only way you'd be negative is if you expressed your feelings with anger or disrespect.

To make this idea clear, let's take a look at several negative ways of expressing concerns. Then we'll show you some much better alternatives.

Negative Ways to Express Concerns

Our work with thousands of couples has shown that there are four forms of communication that can fuel partners' anger and lead to negative behavior.

Mind Reading

Just like a magician, you may be *sure* you know what your partner is thinking or what's behind his or her behavior. Sometimes this mind reading can be a good thing. For example, your wife may have gone to a movie with some friends and come home in a very cheerful mood. To share some of her pleasure and start a friendship talk, you might say, "It looks like you had a great time at the movie." You assume from her happy behavior that she's had fun with her friends. Or maybe, because of your many visits to the local ice cream shop, you know how much your fiancée loves mint chocolate chip ice cream. If you surprise her with some, it's probably safe to assume she's going to gobble it up. Most likely she'll be pleased that you "read her mind."

Often, though, mind reading provokes anger. That's because the person doing the mind reading assumes things that may not be true, which can hurt or anger both the other person and the mind reader. It's also because mind reading often involves making negative interpretations, which, as we told you in Hour 1, is particularly damaging.

Mind reading can cause trouble in two different ways: by being expressed to your partner or by fanning negative flames in your own mind. Say, for example, that your husband missed your first speech to a local business group. Even though he might have had car trouble or another legitimate reason, you might remember that he had been concerned when you decided to change careers. Then you might mind-read the cause of his lateness and say angrily, "You never support me in the things I want to do." Or you might decide not say anything, but be unable to let the incident go. Then you might think to yourself, "He never supports me." And get angrier and angrier.

Mind reading can happen when partners don't share their feelings and thoughts. If partners don't know each other well and don't know what to think, they may project their worst thoughts onto the situation.

Character Assassination

Have you ever witnessed an ugly scene like this? A small child runs into a candy rack at the grocery store, knocking dozens of candy bars to the floor. The stressed-out parent grabs the child and yells, "You're so stupid! How could you do this again?" That's a classic example of character assassination: pinning a negative label on a person rather than dealing constructively with a problem behavior. Instead of saying, "When you run in a store, accidents can happen" or "When you run in the store, I get upset and worried," this parent told the child he always acts stupidly.

Character assassination causes anger and hurt because it forces the attacked person into a corner. It states forcefully that the person has a bad character and that it's not likely to change. And although character assassination can sometimes just slip out in the heat of a fight, it's often done on purpose. We've seen in our work that when couples get upset, they don't so much say what they really believe as much as what they think will help them win an argument or hurt their partner.

Catastrophic Interpretations

"You always have to have the last word." "You never want me to have a good time." Statements like these that use "always" or "never" make generalized, devastating points that are usually wrong. Instead of addressing one behavior or issue, such statements address all of a person's actions in one negative swoop.

Catastrophic interpretations cause anger and pain because they usually cause escalation. One partner makes a catastrophic interpretation, and the other partner responds with a negative statement of his or her own. Pretty soon tempers are flaring and both partners—and the partnership—get hurt.

Blaming

Pinning a problem on someone else is easy to do. None of us likes to take the blame for something that went wrong. But finger pointing is usually done with hostility, and provokes anger. "You forgot to put gas in the car." "It's your fault we were late to the wedding." "This wouldn't have happened if you hadn't messed up." Placing blame is ugly and hurtful, and can cause negative interpretations, escalation, and defensiveness. It also prevents you from working as a team, pushing you apart rather than drawing you together.

Positive Ways to Express Concerns

If none of the four negative patterns we've just described are part of your relationship, three cheers for your team! You're doing your best to discuss concerns with a positive attitude and are treating your partner with respect. You're also taking responsibility for solving problems, rather than expecting your partner to bear the full load.

If any of the negative patterns sound a little too familiar, though, you can stop being part of them right now. Use the following approaches to express and discuss concerns in a positive, caring way.

• *Treat your partner with respect.* Do you yell at your boss when you disagree about a business issue? Do you make a catastrophic interpretation when your friend forgets to phone? Most likely not. You probably express your concern with respect and care. Do the same with the partner you love. By showing respect and consideration, your discussion is much more likely to be positive, and the outcome constructive.

• *Be specific.* Try to say exactly what you think and feel, instead of making generalizations. Then you can concentrate on just the one issue, instead of trying to solve every problem at once. Also be sure you say what *you* think, rather than what you think your partner thinks. You may know a lot about your spouse, but you can't know what he or she is thinking at that moment.

• *Use X-Y-Z statements.* In the last hour we covered X-Y-Z statements in depth, but they're so great for griping constructively that we want to include the structure again here:

"When you do X in situation Y, I feel Z."

The X-Y-Z statement is excellent because it does a number of positive things:

- It names a specific problem to focus on, rather than all problems.
- It acts as a motivator for change and implies that change can take place.
- It names a specific setting, not all settings.
- It names a specific feeling, not all feelings.
- It allows the speaker to own his or her feelings and reactions.
- It allows the speaker to control the expression of feelings.
- It puts emphasis on what the speaker sees and feels rather than on blaming the partner.

All these factors combine to make the X-Y-Z statement a wonderful vehicle for bringing up issues in a positive way. They also allow you to give positive feedback in a specific, caring way. For example, instead of saying, "That was a good back rub," you could put your thanks in the form of an X-Y-Z statement: "When you gave me that back rub last night, I felt wonderful and loved." Which words would you rather hear?

⚡ POWER-UP EXERCISES

INDIVIDUAL EXERCISE

Take out your notebook and think and write about what in this hour had the greatest effect on you.

COUPLE EXERCISE

Go over the ground rules together one rule at a time. Then ask yourselves the following questions to see how each rule will benefit you. Modify any rules you need to so that they'll help you the most.

1. What are the positive things about this ground rule? Are there any negatives?
2. What do we like about this ground rule? What don't we like?
3. How can we rewrite this ground rule to better suit our relationship?

If you modify any ground rules, write down your personalized versions. Then agree to follow the rules for a specific length of time and fix a date to follow up. Adjust the rules again if you need to.

REACHING SECOND

*W*elcome to the second part of the PREP 12-hour program! We want to start this section by congratulating you on how far you've come already. By completing Part One, you've made it to first, and now you're speeding on your way to second. It's looking like your team is going to score!

We know the work in Part One was challenging. Learning to use new techniques for talking safely and new approaches to handling conflict isn't easy. But we also know that you're determined to do your all to have a great and lasting marriage. Keep up the good work!

Now that you've read Part One and learned our research-tested ways to deal with conflict—how to take a positive approach, talk safely and clearly, handle your issues, solve problems, and follow the ground rules for a great relationship—we want to tell you about the importance of making positive connections. Having a great marriage isn't only about knowing how to work through the problems. (And aren't we glad about that!) A lot of it has to do with connecting and sharing: enjoying fun and intimacy together, both sensual and sexual, and creating and sharing important, life-shaping beliefs and visions for the future.

In Part Two we're going to talk about those three major subjects: fun, physical intimacy, and core beliefs. We're going to show you how you can strengthen your relationship and deepen your love by connecting positively in physical, emotional, and spiritual ways.

HOUR 6

Having Fun

SOMETIMES IT CAN SEEM THAT MARRIAGE IS ALL WORK AND NO PLAY. But if
we want our relationship to be loving and strong, we need to concentrate on handling all the hard stuff. So, yes, we spend a lot of time
working out differences and reducing conflict. That's extremely important, as you've learned in the first five hours of this program. But if we
spend all our energy making that effort, along with all the other things
we need to do—earn a living, take care of children, homes, pets, and
ourselves—we're not going to have time to enjoy all the good stuff
marriage has to offer.

That's not a good thing. In fact, having fun is enormously important
to marital health and happiness. In one recent survey, couples reported
that having fun together had the greatest bearing on their overall marital
satisfaction. Another survey told us that the amount of fun partners had
was the most important factor in their commitment and their sense of
friendship. New research under way at the University of Denver

indicates that taking part in leisure activities is very important to how happy partners are in their marriage.

Think back to when you and your spouse started dating. Did you go to the movies? Out to eat? Did you go for walks and hold hands? Did you think there wasn't anything better than spending an evening together, just the two of you? Did you laugh and smile a lot? Did you act silly? Did you talk all night?

Probably you did. Probably having fun was a major part of your relationship.

Now think about last month. Did you and your partner share a lot of fun times? How many dates did you have, with no one else along? Do you remember laughing together over something really crazy? Did you go on a walk, play miniature golf, share burgers and a video, or hang out in the bookstore?

If you can think of several times when you played together and really had fun, your team is on a roll. You're doing a great thing for your relationship, and we encourage you to keep finding the time for enjoyment.

If you thought hard and then said, "Date? Did we have any dates? Are you kidding?" don't worry. Even if fun may have faded to the back burner in your relationship, we're going to show you how to bring it front and center.

A Few Thoughts About Fun

I like nonsense, it wakes up the brain cells.

—AUTHOR THEODORE GEISEL (DR. SEUSS)

All work and no play makes Jack a dull boy.

—COMMON SAYING

Laughter is the shortest distance between two people.

—COMPOSER AND PIANIST VICTOR BORGE

To get the full value of joy you must have somebody to divide it with.

—AUTHOR MARK TWAIN

The most wasted of all days is one without laughter.

—POET E. E. CUMMINGS

Time you enjoyed wasting is not wasted time.

—POET T. S. ELIOT

Time's fun when you're having flies.

—ACTOR KERMIT THE FROG

WHY DON'T WE HAVE FUN?

Early in our relationships, most of us seem to have lots of time for fun. We put a high priority on getting to know each other, and we do that by talking, going out to dinner, and doing activities together that we like. Having fun comes naturally. It's an expected, important part of the dating process.

Then, after marriage, things change. Instead of spending much of the time playing and laughing, we find ourselves working—on our marriage, our careers, our children, our home, and all the other serious parts of our lives. If we stop to think about it, we may discover that we're just not having fun like we used to. And that lack of enjoyment may be putting stress on our marriage by lessening our marital satisfaction.

When fun starts taking a back seat, it's often a result of one of three things: we've gotten too busy, we think we're too grown up for fun (or we only have fun with our kids), or conflict is taking up most of our time.

We're Too Busy to Have Fun

We hope a jam-packed lifestyle hasn't taken all the fun out of your relationship. It definitely affects many couples across the country. Take, for example, Keiko and Kenji. When they first met, they were both in their last year of college. Although they had a lot of studying to do, they often did it together, and took study breaks over sandwiches and coffee. On weekends they went to the beach together, to sporting events, to school parties and activities, or out for pizza and a movie. Sharing things they enjoyed and being constantly in touch were important parts of getting to know each other and falling in love.

About a year after graduating, Keiko and Kenji married. By then both of them had found jobs, and soon after the wedding they bought a condo about 45 minutes from the city where they worked. About a year after that, they had a baby. To be with their new daughter, Keiko decided to quit her job and start a part-time business from home. Kenji found a new job that paid more but was further away.

Everything seemed to be going along fine. Both Keiko and Kenji were crazy about their new baby and loved being parents. Kenji did well at his new job, and Keiko worked hard in every free moment to get her business off the ground. They loved each other and were happy being a family. But after a while, both of them began to feel that life just wasn't as joyful as it used to be. Something good seemed to have slipped away.

What had changed was that fun was no longer a big part of their relationship. They were both working hard, and spent all their free time taking care of the baby and their house. They didn't go out as a couple anymore or spend time at home just talking or doing something enjoyable. Their lives had become so filled with careers, commuting, child care, and housework that there wasn't any space to fit in fun as a twosome.

Like Keiko and Kenji, many couples let the necessities of their busy lives crowd out the fun and playfulness they used to share. In a poll we took, couples on average had gone nearly two months without having a date. And couples who were married between 6 and 20 years went even longer. This may not seem very long to you if you're snowed under by "life," but to us it's a sign that those couples weren't sharing enough fun. And when fun is off the agenda, happiness and satisfaction can follow.

Fun Is for Kids (or Just for Having with Kids)

Experts tell us that having fun and playing are the work of children. By playing, kids develop social, emotional, and reasoning skills and learn to function as separate beings.

We definitely agree with that concept. But we also believe, from what we've seen in our research and workshops, that fun continues to play an important developmental role throughout our lives. In adulthood, play encourages and strengthens the bond between people. It allows us to connect in deep and significant ways. That's because when we're having fun, we're usually more relaxed and more ourselves. And those conditions allow us to fall in love.

That's what happened with Keiko and Kenji. When they were dating in college, they often studied outside, and ended up running around on the lawn, chasing each other and playing Frisbee. They'd fall on the grass and laugh. In fact, they played like kids. By doing fun and crazy things they got to know each other, because they were able to be themselves.

Now that they have a daughter and lots of new responsibilities, Keiko and Kenji are no longer playing together. They do try to fit in some exercise, but it's always alone and it's always haphazard. Kenji does weight training at the gym on days when he doesn't have to stay too late at his office, and Keiko does aerobics with an exercise tape if the baby takes a nap. They get in a little conditioning, but they don't have the easy fun and relaxed activity they used to enjoy as a couple.

Once you have your own children, you can feel as though you always need to be the grownup. Or you may be happy to play with your kids but not think it right or necessary to play with your partner.

Much of the time you do need to be the grownup. But we encourage you to spend time playing too. Definitely play with your children. But have fun and relax with your spouse as well. Playing is great for building adult bonds and keeping joy in your marriage. And that's not only great for you but also one of the best things you can do for your children.

Conflict Gets in the Way

In Part One of this program, we showed you how destructive conflict can be. When it isn't handled well, it can chip away at all the good things the two of you share. And when it chips away at your fun, it can lead to unhappiness and dissatisfaction.

One couple we know, Ruben and Deanna, seemed to be making certain that fun would stay a big part of their marriage. They regularly went out to clubs together and often took classes on subjects they both enjoyed. Though they had children and full-time careers, they made date nights a priority.

On paper that looks great. But in reality date nights often didn't go well. Even though Ruben and Deanna planned to have fun, a small event would often trigger an issue that ruined their entire night.

One night, for example, they took a salsa dance class together. It was fun in the beginning, and the music was great. But after a while, Deanna realized that the female instructor always chose Ruben to demonstrate a step with. Ruben seemed pleased. But when he told Deanna what a great dancer the instructor was, Deanna said angrily, "Why don't you ever tell me I'm a good dancer?"

Then Ruben got angry too, and hardly spoke to Deanna for the rest of the evening. What should have been a fun time together was destroyed because hidden issues were triggered. Deanna had been worrying that Ruben didn't care about her as much as he used to. And Ruben had been feeling that Deanna was always critical of his friends. When the instructor chose Ruben to demonstrate dance steps—because he was such a good dancer—issues that Deanna and Ruben had been afraid to address jumped out to spoil their good time.

As we've said before, conflict affects everyone. But if you deal with it during couple meetings or when both of you are ready and able to talk, it won't be able to destroy your fun. Use one of the techniques discussed in Part One of this book to handle issues during your meetings. If conflict erupts during times meant for fun, as it did for Deanna

RELATIONSHIP QUIZ

Does fun play an important part in your partnership? Think about the following questions.

1. When was the last time you and your partner had a real date, just the two of you having fun together? Men tend to think it's been more recently than women. What do you make of that?

2. What do you think of as a date? Is it only when you go out together for the evening? Or can a date be an afternoon walk, watching a TV show together, or playing cards in the kitchen?

3. Was your last date completely enjoyable? Or did issues or problems spoil part of it?

4. Think back to when you first started going out together. What were the activities you enjoyed the most? Do you still do those things today?

5. Is there a time each week that you've set aside for fun? If you don't have a regular time, what can you do to arrange one?

and Ruben, call a Time Out and talk about the problem later. Fun times need to be exactly that. Conflict should never be allowed to intrude.

KEEPING FUN ALIVE

If you feel like all the fun is draining out of your marriage, or if you want to make sure that doesn't happen, there are several things you can do. Try these suggestions to see what works best for you. By upping your fun time, you'll be strengthening your love.

Make the Time to Play

For some couples, just realizing how important it is to have fun will be enough to start them having more of it. If that's you and your spouse, you'll be on the lookout for times in your schedules when the two of you can pick up a video and share it with only a bowl of pop-corn. Or, before you begin cleaning up the dinner dishes and putting the kids to sleep, you'll remember to fit in a story about something funny that happened at the office. You'll look for times you can say, "Let's forget about raking up the leaves for a while and go for a walk instead." You'll keep fun in the picture with small pleasures and spon-taneous moments.

That's a great start. But to make fun an even bigger part of your married life, it's also a good idea to have larger blocks of time for play.

If your life is already busy with meetings and activities, the only way you may be able to find such blocks is to schedule them. That's not too romantic or spontaneous, you may be saying. But if it's the only way to make sure fun happens, just go ahead and mark your calendar. Plan-ning ahead ensures that you do other important things in life, and it will do the same for fun. Isn't a date with your partner at least as important as your son or daughter's soccer game or a meeting with a client?

If you need to arrange for a baby-sitter for an evening out, then do it at the same time you schedule your date. Choose someone you know and can count on so you'll be relaxed and unworried when you head out the door.

Once you're ready for the good times to roll, make sure you make those times as distraction free as possible. For instance, if you usually wear a beeper, arrange to leave it behind on your dates. Turn off your cell phone, or agree to answer it only in an emergency. If you stay at home, turn on the answering machine and decide not to answer the door. Try to make your time together truly a time for just the two of you.

One thing to remember: because people are usually so busy, it can take a bit of time to wind down and relax on a date. Don't panic if this happens. For instance, if you go away for the weekend, don't worry if one or both of you has difficulty at first switching from everyday-life mode to fun mode. After just a little while, the pleasure of being together and the chance to relax and play will probably make you wonder why you don't make even more time for it.

Be a Kid

Much of the time, we need to act like adults. We have jobs to do, bills to pay, and families, homes, and pets to take care of. We need to be responsible and grown up, in our behavior and our attitude.

When it comes time for fun, though, it's OK to be a little less mature. In fact, engaging in kidlike behavior can be a great way to rekindle your bond and remind yourselves of how you fell in love.

Next time you plan a date, you might want to think beyond a movie or a walk. What did you used to do when you first went out? Think about going bowling, playing miniature golf, or going to the circus or an amusement park. (Don't tell your kids you're going without them!) Have a picnic at the beach or on the back porch. Play board games or cards, ping pong, or video games at the arcade.

Whatever you choose, give yourselves permission to act like a kid. Laugh, smile, tickle, hold hands, chase each other, play catch, see who can toss a grape the highest and catch it in his or her mouth. Do whatever silly thing you used to do that would make both of you laugh. Even if you decide on a more adult date, such as going to a concert or browsing in a bookstore, share some funny stories, flirt a little, and talk like the best of friends.

Protect Fun from Conflict

If you've made the commitment to keep fun in your marriage, you're probably already thinking about the kinds of things you'd like to do. Maybe you've already scheduled some special times for fun. If you have, that's great. In fact, the more the merrier.

Once those times come around, though, you need to make sure that they're filled only with fun. One of the best ways to do that is to refuse to allow conflict to come along.

In Part One we pointed out that conflict likes to spring up at the worst possible times. A very bad time is during an evening meant for fun. Remember Deanna and Ruben? Hidden issues were triggered while they were out for a night of salsa dancing. Their fun was ruined because they hadn't dealt with the issues earlier.

To keep that from happening to you, work on your important issues in meetings arranged for that purpose. Then, when you're out having fun, you won't have to worry that your good time will end in a fight. You'll have a full block of time to laugh, play, and enjoy being together. And having that kind of fun will make your partnership more delightful.

But what if conflict manages to work its way into your date? If you've agreed ahead of time not to let it spoil your fun, you can simply call a Time Out, and talk about the issue at another time. This may be hard to do at first. But once you see how it allows your fun to continue and how it strengthens your relationship, you'll probably find it a good thing to do.

Even when conflict doesn't barge in uninvited, couples are sometimes tempted to bring up issues during their dates. Their reasoning is, We've got this chunk of time for having fun, sure, but let's also take care of some issues.

This thinking is a mistake. Just look at what happened to Shannon and Al when they decided to talk about several important issues while they were out having dinner during an overnight getaway.

> SHANNON: *(smiling and talking happily)* Al, this meal has been so fabulous. I'm stuffed, but I know I'll be able to squeeze in half of that slice of blackberry pie we ordered.

AL: *(taking Shannon's hand across the table)* It has been great, hasn't it. In fact, the whole day has been terrific.

SHANNON: That's for sure. I'm so glad you thought of taking off for the weekend and coming here. I feel so much more relaxed now. The walk this morning was gorgeous, the hotel's beautiful, and I think we're going to find out in a while that the bed's pretty nice too!

AL: *(squeezing Shannon's hand)* I think you're right! We should really get away more often. My mom's always happy to baby-sit.

SHANNON: That does help to keep the cost down. But you know, speaking of cost, I'm wondering if we're going to be able to keep doing things like this if you go back to college for a graduate degree.

AL: Well, I've been thinking about it. Do you want to talk a little bit about it now?

SHANNON: Sure, we've got the time.

AL: Well, I want to do it. In fact, I've sent away for several applications so I can apply to a couple different schools.

SHANNON: *(pulling her hand out of Al's)* You did? You didn't tell me you were definitely going to apply. How much will it cost?

AL: Pretty much. But after I have the degree, I'll be able to get a job at a much higher salary.

SHANNON: *(getting upset)* Yes, but what are we supposed to do in the meantime? I'm only working part-time, and you know I want to have another baby soon.

AL: We can wait a bit for another baby, and maybe you can work some more hours. If I go back to school now, we'll have more money for a bigger family later.

SHANNON: *(more upset)* Well, it sounds like you've got this all worked out, don't you. But I don't happen to agree with you.

> AL: *(seeing their dessert coming, and trying to calm things down)* OK, OK, let's not ruin tonight with another argument. Here's our dessert. Let's talk about this stuff later.
>
> SHANNON: *(throwing her napkin on the table)* You brought it up. And I'm too angry to share anything with you now.

Bringing up issues when you're trying to relax and have fun is a sure way to ruin a good time. Issues are important, but so is time to enjoy yourselves. Each should be given its own space, and each needs your complete attention.

In our experience, one of the best things a couple can do for their relationship is agree to keep conflict out of the time they set aside for fun. In fact, when we first meet with couples who are having problems, we often tell them not to talk about issues, just focus on fun and friendship. When we see them a few weeks later, we generally hear that those weeks have been the best they've had in a long time.

THINGS TO DO FOR FUN

If you've realized how great fun can be for your relationship, you're probably ready to start having your share. If you are, begin by taking these steps:

1. Agree with your partner that you won't let conflict interfere with your fun.
2. Agree on a date and time to set aside for fun. You can set up a regular time or just establish one date.
3. Decide on what you'll do.

For some couples, taking the first two steps is the easy part. Deciding on how you'll spend your time together can be much harder. That may be because you're so unaccustomed to actually having fun. Or it could be because you're not yet sure about the kinds of things you both enjoy.

If you have a hard time coming up with something fun to do, you may want to use the brainstorming technique detailed on page 95. Take out some paper and a pencil and write down all the possibilities. Use your imagination, and accept all ideas without criticism, no matter how silly they sound. (Remember, silly can be good!) You can also think back to the kinds of things you used to do when you first met.

Keeping It Fun

If you already know plenty of ways to have fun, we encourage you to keep having lots of it. And remember these important points:

- Try not to get in a rut. Even if both of you always enjoy going to the movies, try to mix in some other activities. Try going for bike rides, playing checkers, dancing, going out for coffee. Or if you always see adventure movies, test out some romantic comedies. Variety, as they say, is the spice of life.
- Be sure that whatever you do is something you both enjoy. And be sure to take turns choosing the activity.
- Always use friendship talk on your dates. Conflict talk should be avoided and casual talk kept to a minimum. (See pages 71–72 to brush up on the different ways of talking.)
- When you schedule time for fun, don't make it too far off. The sooner you have some fun, the more relaxed and loving you'll feel. Make room for fun now, and have it often.

As you talk and brainstorm, remember that you don't have to come up with extravagant or expensive ideas. Flying to Disneyland and going to see your favorite performer aren't the only ways to have a good time. There are probably a lot of great possibilities to choose from close to home, and many of them will cost little or nothing at all. In fact, you may already have the ingredients for a fun afternoon or evening right at hand: towels and snacks (and maybe pails for building sandcastles) for time at the lake or beach, crayons and colored paper for homemade holiday decorations, music from your teenage years to dance to in the living room, a couch to cuddle on while you watch cartoons or comedy classics.

Still not sure what to do? Here are some suggestions that people we've worked with have come up with over the years. See if one tickles your funny bone or leads you to an idea of your own.

- *Some kind of sport, one you've done already or something that neither of you has tried before:* skiing, jogging, in-line skating, bike riding, horseback riding, tennis, Frisbee, golf, batting cages, bowling, kite flying (you could even make your own kite together), windsurfing, riding scooters, skateboarding, fishing, ice skating, miniature-car racing, rock climbing, spelunking, or trail hiking.
- *A game:* playing a board game (everything from Scrabble to Chutes and Ladders), cards, checkers (regular or Chinese), chess, darts, table tennis, pool, or dominoes, or racing remote-control cars.
- *Some form of entertainment:* going to a movie, a rock or classical concert, the theater, the horse races, the ballet, a car show, a museum or gallery, the circus, the zoo, a fun center, an amusement park, bird or whale watching, a sporting event, or a parade or fair. For places to go, check your local newspaper or search on the Internet. Or you could make your own entertainment. Try singing at a karaoke bar, joining a chorus, dancing (in a style you already know or something new), making a video or a tape, or playing in your own band. Or you could plan a surprise for your partner, something he or she has always wanted to do.
- *Kid stuff:* hopping on pogo sticks, hula hooping, watching cartoons or animated movies, riding dirt bikes, shooting hoops in the driveway, having a food fight (outside, of course!), building sandcastles or snowmen, sledding, running through the sprinklers, going on a roller coaster or down a water slide, painting each other's face or body, or playing tag, catch, a party game (ask your children or your neighbors' children for ideas), or hide-and-seek. Acting like a kid lets the real you shine through—try it!

- *Travel:* Travel is great for having fun, because it carries you away from everyday life and gives you lots of opportunities for adventure. It's also great because going someplace close to home can be just as enjoyable as somewhere far off. Also, travel doesn't have to be expensive. A getaway to the beach or a nearby lake will cost you only gas money. But the change of scene, plus the chance to swim, dunk each other, and sun yourselves, can be invaluable.

When you plan a trip, choose one that fits your interests, or try something completely new. If you like to fish, you could explore a new river or try your hand at ocean fishing. If you want to pamper yourselves, you could book a cruise, for a weekend or longer, or take side-by-side mud baths at a spa. If you'd rather rough it in the great outdoors, think about a rafting trip, a bicycle or walking tour, a rock-climbing adventure in a regional or national park, a ski package, or an overnight at the local campground or in your own backyard.

Some travel companies also offer theme-based travel: mystery trips, adventure trips, educational trips, and activity-based trips, such as those that go to scenic places for artists to paint. Travel agents can help with this kind of trip. Or you can create a less expensive and less involved trip of your own: a walking tour of all the beautiful old houses in a nearby town, or a sports theme trip in which you bicycle to a favorite park, have a picnic lunch and go for a hike, then go home and play table tennis or driveway basketball at night.

Another way you can do some traveling is to extend a business trip. If you travel to another city or country on business, your spouse can meet you there when the business part is over. Then you can both go on to explore the area, following business with pleasure.

- *Miscellaneous fun:* Fun isn't found only by doing special things. There's plenty of fun to be had in the more everyday parts of life. For instance, if you like to cook, make a complete meal of favorites together, then dress up and enjoy it on your best dishes in the dining room. Or try cooking or buying exotic foods and feeding them to each other in the bedroom.

If you like to garden, create a shady spot in your yard for sharing a glass of iced tea and holding hands. Take a drive into the country or the mountains. Cuddle on the front porch swing. Go for a walk in the park or the woods. Take a class together. Read aloud to each other. Make love. Share a bubble bath. Go camping in the back yard. Give each other a back rub. Go shopping and buy each other a tiny gift. Watch home movies from your wedding or a special event. Take in a local site you've never gotten around to seeing. Talk over coffee. Share a gooey chocolate sundae.

MAKING FUN HAPPEN

Once you agree on what you want to do, go right out and do it. Don't say, "That sounds great, let's do it soon," because soon can quickly turn to later if you let it. Make a date to play sometime in the next few days, get a sitter if you need to, and go out and have fun. The idea here is just to spend time together doing something you both enjoy. Once you get the hang of it and make having fun together a priority, we think you'll find that married life becomes a lot more joyful.

⋀ POWER-UP EXERCISES

INDIVIDUAL EXERCISE

Take out your notebook and think and write about what in this hour had the greatest effect on you.

COUPLE EXERCISE

One way to keep fun happening is always to have a big selection of fun-time ideas on hand. Then, whenever there's time for fun, you won't need to wrack your brains for something great to do.

For part of this exercise, we want you to make a deck of cards on which you write down some of your best ideas for having fun. You can think of it as your personal "fun deck." To make your deck you'll need a piece of paper, a package of index cards, and a pen or pencil.

Start by brainstorming as many ways as you can to have fun. Write them all down on the sheet of paper. Be creative and imaginative, and don't hold back. Ideas can cover any topic, be in any price range, and be simple or more complex to do. Anything goes here. The craziest suggestions may turn out to be the best.

When neither of you can think of even one more possibility, choose the best 25 or 30 ideas that both of you like. Include a few that are really special to each of you even if they're not your partner's favorite. Write down each possibility on a separate index card, with any details it may need.

Then, you're ready to choose your activity. Each of you should go through the cards. Pick three cards each that describe things you'd like to do on your next date. When you've made your choices, exchange cards with your partner. Pick one of your partner's cards and have him or her choose one of yours.

Once you've made your choices, each of you is responsible for making your partner's fun activity happen. You can flip a coin to see whose activity goes first if you won't have time to do both on one date. Or you can simply agree to take turns.

Once you've made your plans, there are only two things left to do: go out and have a ball. Then choose new cards and start planning again for the next time!

HOUR 7

Enhancing Your Love Life

AH, LOVE! IT'S THE REASON MOST OF US GET HITCHED. In the early stages of most marriages, sensuality and sexuality are very high priorities. All we want to do is keep touching—to kiss, cuddle, hug, flirt, wrestle a little, have sex, hold hands, make out, whisper, and giggle. And because it's so much fun, we want to keep on doing it.

So why don't couples always keep their love life alive and thriving? We're going to answer that question in this hour and then focus on how you can connect in the wonderful ways of touching. Through intimacy you can come closer together and strengthen your love.

Unfortunately, sensuality and sexuality can lose their top spots on our priority list after the first years of marriage. When the responsibilities of work, home, and family crowd in, we often give less time to showing and sharing love.

In Hour 6 we focused on the importance of keeping fun alive in your marriage. We showed you how having plenty of fun can increase your joy and satisfaction.

Well, sex can do the same thing. In this hour we're going to encourage you to make time for love, and tell you how to keep it safe from anxiety and conflict. We'll show you that by expressing your love physically, through both playful touching and sex, you'll not only increase your pleasure but keep your marriage strong.

THE TWO SIDES OF PHYSICAL INTIMACY: SENSUALITY AND SEXUALITY

For many people, the way to express love physically is to have sex. They show and share love through intercourse, most often (though not always!) in bed.

Having sex is definitely an exciting and wonderful way to show how much you care. But there's another side of physical love: sensuality, or enjoyment received through any of the senses—touching, seeing, smelling, tasting, and hearing. Sensuous acts are things like hugging, holding hands, smoothing your partner's hair, kissing your wife's perfumed throat, running your hand down your husband's bare arm, massaging each other with scented oil, snuggling and listening to soft music, feeding each other chocolate or popcorn, intertwining arms to drink champagne. For some couples it may also include a kind of teasing, wrestling, athletic sensuality. All sensuous acts can happen in bed, but they can also take place in the kitchen, at the beach, or just about anywhere.

Unlike that of sex, the goal of sensuality isn't always intercourse and orgasms, though they can certainly result. Sensual acts can express your attraction and how much you care, and make your partner feel loved, in wonderful, nonsexual ways.

Both sensual and sexual acts are important in marriage because they keep partners from growing apart. But, as we said earlier, both kinds of physical intimacy can diminish over the course of a relationship. Often, though, it's sensuality that drops out of sight first. Because there's less time for love in general, couples tend to save what time there is for having sex.

That can be a problem for two reasons:

1. Couples connect physically only when they make love.
2. It puts pressure on the sexual relationship and can lead to performance anxiety—that is, worrying about how well you're doing when you're making love.

Losing the sensual side of your relationship can also make you less happy. You can literally get too out of touch. Just think about how great you feel when you fool around with your spouse, playing, touching, laughing, giving and getting pleasure. Even when sex isn't in the picture, being sensual with your partner can bring delight and bring you close.

Protecting Your Sensual Relationship

If you and your partner are kissing, cuddling, and caressing as much as you did when you first met, you're doing a great job of seeing that intimacy stays strong in your marriage. Sensuality gives you many ways to express your love physically, and the more you connect physically, the better your relationship will be.

But if you think about the sensuality in your relationship and find that it's lacking, don't worry. You can start to remedy the situation now.

Nicole and Brett are one couple who needed to bring sensuality back to their marriage. Early in their relationship they used to spend a lot of time doing sensual things. Nicole has long wavy hair that Brett loved to stroke and push behind her ears. Sometimes he would wash Nicole's hair when they showered together, and she would wash his back.

They also both loved sports. At the beach they'd play volleyball, and often ended up playfully grabbing each other to win a point. They showed their affection in lots of other ways too: splashing each other while they did the dishes together, holding hands while they walked to their favorite music store, playing hide-and-seek in their apartment, whispering to each other when they danced.

Happily for them, their love grew stronger and stronger. But after a few years of marriage, much of their sensual interaction disappeared. With demanding jobs, a seriously ill parent, and the stress of managing their apartment complex to make extra money, there was little time for and little interest in playful touching.

Still, they loved each other, and continued to have sex. But they were often tired at night, so their lovemaking was usually over quickly. And they managed to have sex just every now and then.

Nicole and Brett still shared physical intimacy. But they were really only having intercourse, not making love.

This began to cause problems. Having a physical connection only during sex made both partners anxious and dissatisfied. Plus Brett thought Nicole was less responsive in bed than she used to be, and he worried about his performance. Nicole missed Brett's loving touches, and wondered if he was losing interest in her.

Luckily, Brett and Nicole used some of our PREP techniques to deal with their problem. Here's how it worked:

Talking It Over

When couples feel that something is not quite right, they can begin to wonder if something major is wrong. Happily for Brett and Nicole, they made an appointment to talk about their worries during a couple meeting. By choosing a time when they were both calm and ready to talk, they were able to confront the problem and keep it from being triggered at a bad time.

During their couple meeting, the two partners used the Speaker-Listener Technique to express what they were feeling. In that way they made sure that each heard the other's viewpoint. As they talked, they discovered that the loss of nonsexual physical intimacy was hurting their relationship. But they were also reassured to hear that they were both still very much in love.

Brett and Nicole arranged a fairly formal meeting to talk about their problem. But it's also possible to hold this kind of talk less formally. If you choose to do so, agree to have a safe and honest exchange in which you both respect each other's point of view. Express your feelings in a way that doesn't threaten or attack your partner.

Agreeing on a Solution

Once they discovered what the problem was, Brett and Nicole brainstormed things they could do to increase their physical closeness. They talked about the kinds of sensual things they each liked and what they could do to carve out time to do them. Some things they set aside specific time for. For example, they decided that cuddling on the couch for 10 or 15 minutes after dinner each night wouldn't take much time from all the things they had to do, but it would give them a chance to relax, put their arms around each other, and share some special words. They decided that neither of them would bring up an issue during those times, that they would reserve the time only for connecting and feeling good.

Other sensual things that Nicole and Brett decided to do were put into an "as often as possible" category. Nicole told Brett how much she had loved it when he stroked her hair. Brett said how much he had liked it too, and that he would remember to touch her hair often. Brett said he would love it if Nicole massaged his shoulders when they got into bed, and she promised she would do that as much as possible. Without making lots of strict rules about being sensual, which might have made them even more anxious than they had been, they agreed to pay more attention to the little touches and pleasures they both liked.

Watching Out for "Solutions" That Aren't Discussed First

Nicole and Brett handled their problem in a great way. They discussed the issue, then discussed solutions, then committed to making things better and being the best sensual partners they could be, both individually and as a team. (Being sensual is definitely a team sport!)

Blanca and Mike didn't handle their problem as well. Like Brett and Nicole, they didn't spend much time touching each other in nonsexual ways. They also started having difficulty in bed, because they wanted to be close but only connected during sex. The couple felt pressured to make love, and could never relax.

Soon Mike realized that Blanca wasn't enjoying their lovemaking as much as she used to. He thought he wasn't satisfying her, and decided he'd try to please her more. At the same time, Blanca felt that Mike didn't care about her as much as he had and was only using her sexually. She began to resent the fact that he always had orgasms, and she had them only every now and then.

Thinking he would make Blanca happier, Mike initiated sex more often. He also tried some new techniques. Blanca did seem more satisfied for a while and was able to have more orgasms. But Mike always felt tense when they made love, because he worried that he wouldn't be able to make Blanca happy. Even though Blanca enjoyed feeling more pleasure, she still felt somewhat used because the only time Mike touched her was in bed. And in bed there was no feeling of closeness or affection, just the sexual act.

Mike and Blanca didn't solve their problem, because they never discussed the issue and never worked together on a solution. Instead, Mike took it on himself to handle the problem the way he thought it should be done, and Blanca kept her unhappiness and resentment to herself.

Their problem continued until the couple followed Brett and Nicole's lead. Once they started talking more safely and clearly about it, they were able to uncover and later solve the problem. Then, by continuing to communicate and staying committed to their plan, they brought sensuality back to their relationship. This not only brought joy to their marriage but also brought better sexual experiences.

Sensual Talking

One of the best ways to enhance your sensual relationship is through what we call *sensual talking*. That means telling your spouse how sexy she is, how crazy you are about him, how excited you get when you touch her, how you can't wait to get him in bed. Sensual talking includes any kind of message that tells your partner about your love.

One great way to talk sensually is to whisper something affectionate or hot into your partner's ear. You can do this when you're out on a date or when you're doing the dishes or getting ready for bed. Any time is a good time for telling your spouse how attracted you are.

Sensual talking can also be done when you're apart. For instance, you can leave a loving or provocative message on your spouse's voice mail (just be sure no one else has access to it). Or you might want to send a sexy e-mail message (again, only if no one else can read it). Research shows that engaging in sensual talk when there's no immediate possibility of having sex leads to a better sexual connection later on.

Sensual messages can also be accompanied by a token of your love. A single flower, a balloon, or a tiny gift can add to your mate's pleasure.

Protecting Your Sexual Relationship

In addition to keeping your sensual relationship strong, the two of you also need to have a satisfying sexual connection. Through the physical act of love you not only give and receive pleasure but also strengthen your partnership on a very profound level.

To keep your intimate moments something you look forward to and enjoy, you need to protect them from two destructive things: performance anxiety and conflict.

Performance Anxiety

Performance anxiety is worry about how well you're doing when you make love to your spouse. You think, "Am I making him happy?" "Am I doing this right?" "Is she getting excited?" "Should I be doing something else?" "Am I as good as her old lover?" When you're supposed to be sharing enjoyment, you're feeling anxious instead. And being anxious is a sure way to become less aroused and less able to please your partner.

Think back to the problem Mike and Blanca had. When they started to have trouble in bed, Mike thought it was because he wasn't making Blanca happy. That made him feel worried and tense, and took away the pleasure of making love to her. And Mike's focus on his performance made Blanca feel used.

Performance anxiety can lead to other problems as well. It can cause you to feel distant while making love, as though you're watching instead of participating. This kind of detachment can cause everything from sexual boredom to premature ejaculation to problems maintaining an erection or becoming lubricated to trouble having an orgasm. It's just about impossible to worry and feel aroused and lovingly connected at the same time.

To prevent performance anxiety and all its problems, don't do what Blanca and Mike did. Instead, follow these suggestions:

- Don't rush your intimate moments. Give yourselves plenty of time to relax into having sex, and plenty of time to make each other happy in ways you enjoy.
- Remind yourself to relax. Remember, this is supposed to be fun! If you have trouble relaxing, try taking a warm bath ahead of time, touching each other sensually first, or doing something else that makes you feel good.
- Stay in the moment and replace any negative thoughts with positive self-talk. For example, don't think about being rejected but about how good you feel and how good you can help your partner feel. Some people don't initiate sex because they're afraid it won't go well.
- Use sensual talking to show your partner that you're happy with what he or she is doing (see page 148 to review). Loving whispers or suggestions will help turn you both on and increase your satisfaction.
- Talk about your sexual issues at a couple meeting or at another time you set aside. Use the Speaker-Listener Technique so that

both of you have the chance to say how you feel. The key is not to address your problems during lovemaking or other pleasurable times.

Conflict

In Part One of this book we talked a lot about how destructive conflict can be outside the bedroom. It can also be big trouble for your physical relationship. Many couples say that when they've been arguing and angry with each other about nonsexual issues, they definitely don't feel like making love. Conflict can even halt your lovemaking if the act triggers an unresolved issue. Worry about triggering an issue can prevent you from starting.

Some couples do find that their sexual relationship is actually enhanced following conflict, because having sex is one of the ways they make up. But the positive effects of this kind of solution are usually temporary, and conflict returns.

So what can you do to protect your sexual connection from the destructive forces of conflict? Here are several critical things:

- Agree to keep problems and disagreements strictly off-limits during intimate times.
- Set specific, nonsexual times to discuss issues and then to solve them.
- Follow the ground rules in Hour 5 and use the techniques for handling conflict in Part One.

Making love with your partner is a powerful way to draw closer and show how much you care. Keeping conflict out of the bedroom will help make that happen.

Low Sexual Desire

This may come as a surprise to you: many experts believe that the biggest problem couples will face during the next several decades is a decreasing interest in sex. Sex therapists are already seeing this happen: many say that the most common complaint they hear from couples is that one of the partners has no interest in having sex. One recent study of sexual problems also reported that 43 percent of the women and 31 percent of the men had some kind of significant sexual problem. Of these people, 5 percent of the men and 22 percent percent of the women had low sexual desire. Another 14 percent of the women said they felt desire but had trouble becoming sexually aroused.

Having little interest in sex can be the result of a number of different things. Some of the key ones are

- Depression
- Side effects from medication
- Excessive use of alcohol
- Having a medical problem, such as erectile dysfunction or vaginitus
- Having a chronic disease
- Boredom
- Experiencing hormone-related problems
- Stress
- Having trouble sleeping
- Being tired

If you or your partner is experiencing low sexual desire, the first thing to do is see a doctor. Get a complete checkup and talk about the problem. Be sure to mention if you're suffering from one of the factors listed above.

Although you may think that talking to your doctor about sex will be embarrassing, his or her expertise may do a lot to solve the problem. And if you can begin to enjoy lovemaking again and want to do it often, you'll be very glad you talked about your concerns.

If your partner is the one with low sexual desire, be sure to be supportive as he or she works through the issue. Pressure and anger will not help at all.

If physical or medical problems are ruled out, or if one of the factors we listed is the cause and will take time to remedy, work together on things that can be improved. Here are some ideas:

- Talk openly about sensual and sexual acts that are likely to bring pleasure. Don't be embarrassed to say what you'd really like. Remember, you're talking to someone who's on your side.
- Try some of the suggestions at a time when you're both relaxed and won't feel rushed. Sensual talking and sensual touching may be a good way to start.
- Be patient and understanding. If you're the one with the issue, don't let it make you completely miserable. Give yourself time. If your partner has little desire, keep showing your love and be encouraging.
- Read self-help books on the subject. Most bookstores will have a variety of sex-related guides that can give you new insight into the problem.
- See a sex therapist. If nothing you try helps, you may want to contact a certified sex and marital therapist for expert advice and information.

If both of you have little interest in sex, the situation may not be a problem for your relationship, although both of you would be missing out on a special way of connecting. But if one of you has normal or high interest and one of you has little or none at all, the difference can cause a lot of pain. This is especially true if physical intimacy is one of the main ways you feel connected. But working together as a team will increase your chances of improving sexual desire and keeping it at an exciting level.

RELATIONSHIP QUIZ

Think about the following questions.

1. What comes to mind when you think of the word *sensual?*
   List at least three feelings, activities, or objects.
2. What comes to mind when you think of the word *sexual?*
   List at least three feelings, activities, or objects.
3. Think about how often you and your spouse talk sensually.
   Is it part of your intimate relationship? Think about how you
   might do more of it to enhance your physical intimacy.
4. Think about how often you and your partner are sensual
   with each other. Does sensual touching and talking always
   lead to sex? Or are there times when you touch each other
   playfully or lovingly without anticipating sex?
5. Has conflict ever interrupted your lovemaking? Was there
   anything you could have done to stop it?
6. Think about your level of interest in having sex. Would you
   say it matches your partner's?

COMMUNICATING DESIRE

Talking about sex can be a difficult thing to do. We're afraid that something we say might embarrass our mate or ourselves. Or cause anger or defensiveness. Or make us blush or stammer. Or something we say might be misunderstood, and lead to more embarrassment or conflict.

But talking about your physical relationship is an important way to protect it. Communicating clearly and honestly will not only help you handle potential conflicts about sex but also let both of you know what your partner desires.

Telling Your Partner What You Like

Sometimes, especially after they've been together for a while, partners begin to assume things about each other. That's fine if it's about something like books: you've seen your spouse read a ton of mysteries, so you can be pretty sure she'd love one for a gift.

It also can be fine about your physical relationship. For instance, if your husband has told you several times that he loves a particular thing you do in bed, it's pretty safe to assume that he'll like it when you do it again.

It would be a mistake to assume, though, that he likes everything that you like. Or even that he'll always like something he enjoys now. People change and circumstances change. So it's important for both of you to check in often about your sexual desires.

But, you may be thinking, we've been together for decades. By now my partner should know what I like and don't like!

That's not a reasonable expectation. Sure, your partner probably knows a lot about what makes you happy. But your partner isn't a mind reader. He or she can't always know what would give you pleasure unless you say so.

But, you say again, how unromantic is that? Right in the middle of making love I'm supposed to stop and say, "Yes, that's good. No, do this instead"?

The answer is yes (though you don't have to stop!). But you'll want to do this in a way that works well for both of you. For example, we encourage you to say clearly and lovingly exactly what feels good to you while you're touching or making love. It doesn't have to be a major dialogue. Just talk or whisper together about what turns you on, what isn't working, what you'd like to do. This can be exciting in itself, but it will also let you know how to make your partner happy. And it will keep you from making assumptions that might be wrong.

You can also talk about desires during nonintimate times. Then you'll be able to hear each other clearly, without distractions. And you may find that talking about what you like soon leads to doing what you like.

Research has shown that couples who have great long-term physical relationships have learned to talk safely and honestly about what brings them pleasure. This includes talking with their bodies as well as their words. Research has also shown that couples who have joyful intimate relationships also have a real desire to please their partner.

Taking Risks

Talking about what you like and don't like is a great way to improve and protect your lovemaking. It also helps to try some new things. If you've been together for some time, your sexual habits may have gotten a bit predictable.

But expressing your fantasies and wants can be scary. By talking about them openly you risk being rejected. You also make yourself vulnerable by showing who you are. We've learned, though, that couples who have great sex are able to overcome their fears and talk about their desires.

The Speaker-Listener Technique can help with this kind of discussion. Eric and Elissa used it to talk safely about adding new pleasure to their lovemaking.

> ERIC (Speaker): I've been afraid to talk about this before, but I've been wanting to try something different when we have sex.
>
> ELISSA (Listener): You want to try something new when we make love, but you've been worried about telling me.
>
> ERIC (Speaker): That's right. I know your family doesn't show affection a lot, and I think it's hard for you to talk about sex.
>
> ELISSA (Listener): You think it's hard for me to talk about what you want because my family isn't very open about that kind of thing.
>
> ERIC (Speaker): Yeah. But I'd really like to have sex in the shower and in front of the fireplace. Lots of different places, instead of always in bed. It's great making love with you in bed. But I think it could be really exciting if we did it where we got started, or tried some places that might be hot.

ELISSA (Listener): You like to make love with me, but you think doing it in different places could be more exciting.

ERIC (Speaker): That's it. What do you think? *(He gives Elissa the piece of carpet they use to show who's the Speaker.)*

ELISSA (Speaker): I'm glad you brought this up. I really like making love with you too, but it is hard for me to talk about sex stuff.

ERIC (Listener): You're happy we're talking about this even though it's hard for you. And you like making love with me. I'm really glad about that.

ELISSA (Speaker): Yes, that's it. And I'm glad too. And maybe we are missing out on something by always having sex in bed. I guess I've always thought that was right because of the conservative way I was brought up. I guess I'm a little shy about this stuff.

ERIC (Listener): You've been thinking that having sex in bed was the only place we should do it. But now you're thinking that we might be missing out on something good by not trying other places.

ELISSA (Speaker): That's right. Do you want to tell me about some of the places you think would be exciting?

Talking about your physical relationship is the first important step in improving it. Then you need to go ahead and try some of the things you discuss. When you talk and experiment,

- Be honest about your desires.
- Talk sensitively with your spouse about his or her wants. If you don't want to try something, say so. But say it kindly, and try to suggest an alternative.
- Read a book or watch a video about sex together. Try something new described or shown in it.

- Be creative. Explore different sensual and sexual techniques and talk about what turns you on.
- Agree to surprise each other on a certain night with something new.
- Be encouraging and loving. Pressure, criticism, and anger won't bring pleasure to either of you.

Remember Romance

As you explore new ways to enhance your intimacy, don't forget about romance. Tender and passionate words and actions can quickly put the love back in your lovemaking.

- Do romantic, sensual things. Send a single flower or a bouquet, call in the middle of the day to say "I love you," touch your spouse erotically, slip a loving note into a pocket, surprise your partner with a small gift or a special night out, go for a walk in the rain, book a room at a local hotel for an hour or a night, hold hands wherever you go.
- Instead of taking your partner's love for granted, focus on winning his or her love and affection. Be helpful, tender, considerate, and giving. Look and be your best. Show your esteem as well as your desire.
- Be sensitive to your partner's rhythms, wishes, and needs. For example, if she enjoys early-morning sex but you're a night person and like to make love late in the evening, push yourself to adapt to her sensual times.
- Take risks and be creative. Initiate lovemaking at unexpected times and in unexpected places. Try new positions and techniques. Be the initiator if your spouse usually gets things started.
- Be a great lover. Kiss and touch in ways and places that excite and satisfy your partner. And let your partner know how happy it makes you to receive his or her expressions of love.

MAKING PHYSICAL INTIMACY A PRIORITY

Many experts believe that sexual chemistry decreases over time. While this may be true for some people, it doesn't have to mean that the love and attraction you feel for your mate will inevitably fade. In fact, we're certain that the reason most couples fall out of love isn't because of chemistry. It's because they don't invest enough time each day in friendship, fun, and their physical relationship. By building and nourishing those connections, you can build and sustain your love.

Yes, we know you're busy. All sorts of things compete for your time and attention. But if your marriage is important to you, it's important to make time for love.

That means you need to agree to make your sensual and sexual life a priority. Make dates ahead of time if you need to. Take every opportunity to show your love and affection. Be romantic and creative. And remember that love isn't expressed only through having sex. It's also shown with a special look, a sexy note, a touch under the table, a whispered "I love you," cuddling and hugging, sharing fantasies, or bringing home flowers "just because." However you choose to show your love, make physical intimacy something you think about and act on often.

ᚺ POWER-UP EXERCISES

INDIVIDUAL EXERCISE

Take out your notebook and think and write about what in this hour had the greatest effect on you.

COUPLE EXERCISE

The following exercise will help you do two things:

1. Focus on keeping sensuality in your relationship
2. Help you talk more openly and naturally about what you like and don't like in your lovemaking

The exercise, called the Sensate Focus, was developed by sexual-relationship experts Masters and Johnson, and has benefited many couples. To do the exercise, you and your partner take turns giving and receiving pleasure.

The Sensate Focus

Whichever of you is the Giver, your role is to give pleasure to your partner by touching him or her and responding to the feedback. Gently touch your partner's body, paying attention to his or her reactions. Ask for feedback as often as you want. And be aware of changes. Something that feels good initially may eventually hurt. As you touch your partner, focus on what he or she wants, not on what you think will feel good.

When you're the Receiver, your role is to enjoy being touched and to give feedback on what feels good and what doesn't. You can provide feedback by telling your partner how you feel and what you'd like. Or you can guide his or her hand to a different area or move it in the way you like to be touched. Give feedback often so your partner learns what feels good to you.

As you take turns being the Giver and the Receiver, follow these guidelines:

- Begin the exercise by having the Giver massage the hands or feet of the Receiver, asking for and giving feedback. Focusing on these less sexual areas will help you relax into the exercise and get the hang of how to do it.
- Switch roles after about 5 or 10 minutes. Switch and repeat as often as you want.
- Don't focus on having the exercise lead to sex. Focus on sensuality and discovering what you both enjoy. If you do want to have sex after the exercise, be sure you both agree to it.
- Do the exercise several times a week for several weeks. Once you're ready, begin touching other areas of your partner's body, including sexual areas, as long as he or she is comfortable with it.

- When you're ready, you can stop switching between Giver and Receiver. Work on giving and receiving pleasure at the same time, but still focus on being sensual and communicating desires.

In addition to setting aside time to do the Sensate Focus exercise, you can keep sensuality strong in your relationship by setting aside time to do specific sensual things together. When you plan for these times, make sure you won't be interrupted. (This is a great time for a baby-sitter or an answering machine!) Talk together about what is sensual for each of you. Here are some possibilities:

- Give each other a back rub or a massage.
- Share fantasies.
- Cuddle as you tell your partner all the things you love about him or her.
- Talk about a sensual or sexual activity you'd like to do the next time you're together.
- Fix a fabulous meal together and then share it by candlelight. Sit close and feed each other bites.
- Make out in your car or in front of the fireplace.
- Take a bath or shower together and wash each other's hair.

Try whatever you like that gets you talking and touching in sensual ways. And have fun and enjoy it!

HOUR 8

Sharing Values and Core Beliefs

DURING THE LAST TWO HOURS, WE'VE SHOWN YOU HOW TO BUILD a great marriage by having a great time together. We've discussed how important it is to have fun and connect intimately, and we've given you lots of ways to do both.

Now we're going to take a look at another powerful way to strengthen your relationship. It's a little more serious, but it can have very positive and lasting effects on your marriage.

What we're going to talk about here we call *core beliefs*. For us these mean religious beliefs, spiritual beliefs, philosophical beliefs, values, cultural practices, worldviews—all the important principles that guide you through your life. Because these beliefs are so fundamental to who you and your partner are, they can have a big effect on your marriage—they can strengthen it or threaten it. We, of course, want your core beliefs to help you achieve a great, lasting marriage. So in this hour we're going to show you how to discuss them openly and draw closer by sharing these parts of your life.

If you're not religious, you may think that you should just skip this hour. But please don't. Yes, we're going to talk about why research on religious involvement and faith shows that people who are more religious have happier marriages. But our goal is to help you by translating research on religion and spirituality into principles you can use to help you and your partner support each other and grow closer together over time. Whatever you think about religion, this hour can help promote stability and love in your relationship.

RELIGION AND SPIRITUALITY

Most people think about religion as a set of principles and practices that members of an organized group follow. When they think about spirituality, they may think about more personal beliefs and experiences of their own. Both religious and spiritual beliefs are part of the core beliefs that guide many people's lives.

Although spirituality is hard for researchers to study because it's more difficult to define, a lot of research has been done on the effects of religious involvement on married couples. Many of the studies, and our own, show that religious involvement is beneficial for most couples. In the following sections, we've distilled these findings into important themes that will help you in your relationship, whether you're religiously inclined or not.

The Positive Effects of Relating Religiously or Spiritually

Research has shown that taking part in religious activities affects most married couples positively in several ways:

- Couples who are more religious tend to be a bit more satisfied with their marriage and less likely to divorce.
- Religious couples have lower levels of conflict and higher levels of commitment than nonreligious couples.
- Religious couples are happier to sacrifice for one another and have a stronger sense of themselves as a couple.

- Religious couples tend to have satisfying and more frequent sex than average.

But it's not that couples who are more religious have dramatically better marriages. Religious involvement appears to give couples an edge, not a huge advantage, in keeping their marriages strong.

A number of research studies suggest, though, that the edge grows significantly when partners practice their faith together. For couples who do so, in any of the many possible ways, it's a powerful element in developing a deeper connection in life.

Couples who actively share in this way tend to be happier, to have less conflict, to work more as a team, and to experience fewer of the danger signs discussed in Hour 1. We think it's a bit easier for religiously oriented couples who have similar core beliefs to develop their shared life in this way. But don't worry if that's not you. As we discuss below, couples in which one or both partners are not at all religious or have different beliefs and practices can also develop their bond by sharing their deeper beliefs with one another.

Finding a Religious Community When You Have Different Faiths

If the benefits of practicing your faith together sound good to you, you may already be thinking of doing it. But if you and your partner observe differently or are of different denominations or different faiths, you may be wondering where to start.

An author and colleague of ours, Joel Crohn, developed a process that should help:

- Begin by acknowledging the differences in your backgrounds. Talk about your upbringing and your connection to your religion.
- Then go on to what Crohn calls *unconditional experimentation*. That means exploring each other's religious beliefs and needs by attending services in a variety of houses of worship, including

those you might have grown up with but also others that neither of you have attended before.

- Next, use the problem-solving approach described in Hour 4 to help you choose the path you both want to take. Thoroughly discuss what you think will and won't work, and where you can compromise. Take particular care to brainstorm lots of possible ways to proceed. After you've made your decision, set a time to follow up.
- Put your plan into practice until the follow-up date. Then discuss how well it has worked and whether or not you're both happy with your choice. If you're not, repeat the process, choosing and exploring a new plan. Keep working until you've found a religious practice that satisfies both sets of needs.

Something for Every Couple, Whether You're Religious or Not

If you're religious or open to becoming religious, everything we've just told you about practicing your faith together may sound great. But what if you're just not religiously or spiritually inclined? We believe that the points we are about to make, which come from research on religious belief and involvements, are relevant to all couples—nonreligious, of different religions, or those who practice the same faith.

Why do we think religious involvement holds some secrets for nonreligious couples? Because we've found two very positive things in the research that we think benefit *all* couples, religious or not:

1. All couples need a support system. They benefit by being more connected to friends and family who can provide emotional or other types of support to help keep their marriage strong.
2. Most couples benefit by sharing and defining core beliefs and, where possible, developing a shared worldview.

Both of these things can make your marriage stronger, happier, and more secure for the long term. Let's take a deeper look at each of them.

THE NEED FOR SOCIAL SUPPORT

Many studies have shown that people who are isolated and not closely connected with family and friends are at greater risk for a number of problems: emotional problems, such as depression and thoughts of suicide; a variety of health and physical problems; and economic problems, including poverty. In fact, recent research tells us that the health risks of isolation are as great as those of smoking. It's just not good for most people to be all alone.

Studies also point out that it's good for people to be part of a social group. People who hook themselves up with others are much less likely to suffer the negative effects of isolation. You and your partner are already part of the same team. But couples who have strong connections with others who know and care about them as a twosome are more likely to do well in marriage than those who are isolated.

Joining a Group

Religion offers many couples a fast track to developing a strong support system. It provides an environment in which there are not only others to connect with but also members who believe that marriage is worth the investment and effort it sometimes requires.

There are also nonreligious ways to become more connected with communities of support. For example, many couples connect by getting involved in groups with others who have similar interests. Here are just a few of the many possibilities:

- Support groups related to having a child or loved one who struggles with a particular difficulty. For example, there are many community-based support groups for those who have a parent suffering from Alzheimer's or a child with a developmental delay.
- Groups that come together around a shared interest in helping the local schoolchildren, such as the PTA or an adult-run program for kids (for example, scouting or a soccer league).

- Groups that come together around a shared interest or hobby, such as those in which members share a passion for ballooning, stock-market investment, books, or travel.

Do you and your partner have a strong network of friends and family who support you? Do you do things with others who encourage you in your life? Do you want to do more, and are you actively doing more, to connect with others as a couple?

Two partners who found joy and support in a religious community are Jorge and Patty. The two met as teenagers when they joined their church youth group. They spent time together on church-sponsored skiing trips, singing in a Christian rock group, and bringing meals to elderly parishioners. And their families often sat together at Sunday morning services.

When Patty and Jorge got engaged, the church community was thrilled. And when they got married, they were supported not only by their families but also by a big network of friends. Everyone who had been involved with them—at church, during activities, and doing volunteer work—wished them well. Through their faith and religious involvement, Patty and Jorge developed a network of people who shared their values and encouraged their commitment. And that has done a lot to strengthen their marriage.

Another couple, Elizabeth and Jonathan, found support in a nonreligious group. Their different religious backgrounds had never divided them, but it had gotten in the way of their being connected in the community. When their first child, Alicia, showed signs of severe developmental problems, their urge to help her pushed Elizabeth and Jonathan to get involved with others for support. The group of parents they found helped them pull together as a couple, gave them a place to fit in, and enabled them to develop relationships that grew into strong friendships based on a shared need for mutual support.

If you're interested in increasing the social support for your own marriage, you might want to look into the network of groups affiliated with the Association for Couples in Marriage Enrichment, or ACME.

ACME is a nonreligious international organization that focuses on helping married couples move through life. The groups encourage couples to get together, share ideas and activities, and help each other out. Many couples we know have found ACME groups a great source of support and a way to have fun and connect with other couples. We have regularly spoken at ACME international conferences, and believe that the people involved are great. You can find out more about this organization by writing to them at P.O. Box 10596, Winston-Salem, NC 27108; calling 336-724-1526 or 800-634-8325; e-mailing acme@marriageenrichment.org; or visiting their Web site at www.bettermarriages.org.

Lending Your Support

One of the ways you and your partner can strengthen your network of support is to do things together for others. For example, you could volunteer your time to a homeless shelter or food bank to give to others who have less. Or you could tutor children who are having trouble reading. Or you could volunteer to help build or repair homes through organizations such as Habitat for Humanity. Whatever your interest, there's a group that would love to have your help. (Check the Yellow Pages for volunteer centers and the newspaper and Internet for organizations looking for volunteers.) Being part of that group would not only allow you to contribute but also provide you with a network of like-minded friends. In addition, these types of activities can be very powerful in drawing the two of you together because they allow you to join with and give to others in ways that can bring depth and added meaning to your lives.

All in the Family

As you look to increase your support systems, don't overlook what may be the greatest one of all: your family. Though some couples don't have family members they can rely on, most do, and they can enrich and support you and your relationship.

In the past, most couples married and had kids and continued to live in the same community they did as children. Now, though, people are less likely than ever before to live near their family. That can make it harder to maintain close family ties. But even if you don't live close to relatives, e-mail and low-cost long-distance calling rates can help you stay connected to loved ones. And if your aunts, uncles, cousins, siblings, parents, or grandparents live close to home, so much the easier. Unless you have really difficult family relationships, see what comes from just a little more effort to reach out to yours as a couple.

SHARING A WORLDVIEW

Connecting with others as a couple is an important way to strengthen and enhance your own bonds. Another way to deepen your connection is to develop and share a worldview. What's a worldview? It's how you understand all of life, including the big questions—the hows and the whys. It involves things like your take on the meaning of life, what's right and what's wrong, what happens after death, what marriage is, what being a parent is, and what things are most important to you.

When couples share the same worldview, we've found that it's easier for them to develop a shared vision of their relationship. This includes their sense of themselves as a couple as well as the goals they have for their partnership. This vision, in turn, helps keep their marriage happy for the long term. Fran Dickson, a communications expert from the University of Denver, found that partners who stayed happily together for 50 years most likely had a shared worldview.

Developing a similar worldview may be a bit easier for couples who practice the same religion. That's because most religious faiths have specific beliefs and standards, including ways in which the major issues are viewed. When you have the same faith and you practice it together, it becomes relatively easier for you to share your views on life.

If you have similar core beliefs, religious or otherwise, have the two of you talked deeply about them? Worldviews and core beliefs go to the very heart of how most people define themselves. Talking regularly about such things in the light of what's going on in your lives can draw you closer together.

Take Care Not to Take Things for Granted

Even if your worldview seems to be pretty much the same as your partner's, it would be a mistake to assume you agree on everything. It would also be a mistake to take for granted what your partner's outlook will be on every issue.

Though you may be in synch on most matters, talking about your viewpoints will make it clear where each of you is coming from. Then, if your views are similar, you can put them into effect as a team. If they're not similar, discussing and understanding them will make them less likely to cause conflict.

It's pretty certain that no matter how close your outlooks generally are, sometimes you and your spouse are going to disagree. Identifying similarities and differences case by case will help you move forward as a team.

Core Values

When both partners believe in the following key values, their marriage usually benefits:

- Being committed to each other
- Having respect for each other
- Sharing intimacy
- Showing forgiveness

These four values have been shown to be associated with good relationships. And research shows that basing a shared worldview on these values is an important way to bring about marital success.

If you think about it, most belief systems, religious or not, promote these values in their codes of conduct and ethics. As you can probably tell, these core values also underlie the approach we present to you throughout these 12 hours. Our years of experience show that when both partners take these values to heart, they become closer and their marriage becomes more enjoyable.

RELATIONSHIP QUIZ

Answer the following questions about each of the four values:

- Being committed to each other
- Having respect for each other
- Sharing intimacy
- Showing forgiveness

1. How did you develop this value? For example, did it come from the way you were brought up, or did a particular experience affect what you believe in?
2. How do you express this value in your behavior toward your partner?
3. How important is this value to your relationship? Is it a necessary part of your relationship? Or does it add something positive, but you can do without it?
4. If it's a necessary part of your relationship, how can you protect it? How can you ensure it's nurtured in your relationship?

Expectations

When you're dealing with the big issues in life—parenting, intimacy, relationships, goals—your core values come into play. When you're coping with day-to-day issues, such as who's going to make dinner, which car you should buy, how much money you should save, or who's going to initiate sex, it is expectations that surface. Your ideas about how things should be done and what you think should happen affect your choices and your marriage.

Studies show that when couples share expectations about key marital issues, they're able to sail more smoothly when the water gets rough. Shared expectations lead to shared practices and routines, which help couples work together as a team.

When partners don't share expectations, the differences can spark conflict. In fact, the possibility of this happening is so great that our program devotes the entire next hour to the subject. But here we want to say that sharing the same philosophy of life makes it easier to share expectations.

HANDLING DIFFERENT WORLDVIEWS

So far we've talked a lot about how beneficial it is when couples share the same worldview. If you and your partner are on pretty much the same wavelength here, you've got a great foundation for a loving, lasting marriage.

But not all couples share the same take on life. You and your partner may have different religious backgrounds, different values, different philosophies or practices, or different expectations. If you do, you may be worried that your relationship is headed for trouble. Or you may be feeling some quiet discontentment or concerns.

For some couples, not sharing the same core beliefs becomes a major risk to their closeness. For others, the ways they handle their differences draw them close together as friends. If you and your partner have very different worldviews that are distancing you, we want to tell you that it doesn't have to be that way. Remember what we said about conflict in the early part of this program? Conflict can kill a marriage. But if you handle conflict well, it can be prevented from doing permanent damage. The same goes for worldviews. If the two of you handle differences in worldviews calmly, honestly, and with respect, those differences won't distance you. In fact, they may end up being a source of closeness and much deeper friendship, because discussing them will give you a chance to learn about each other on a very fundamental level.

Keeping Differences from Hurting Your Marriage

Jeff and Brittany are one couple who kept their different beliefs from hurting their marriage. Both partners grew up in extremely political families, but Jeff was a strong Democrat and Brittany a fervent Republican. Luckily neither one believed in the old advice that if you want to stay friends, never discuss religion or politics.

The longer they were married, the more their politics became involved in their lives. It affected which newspapers they read, which companies they invested in, and of course which political candidates they voted for. They had fundamental differences in how they thought many issues should be handled. When their son became old enough to understand different perspectives, they became concerned about how they could bring him up under two very different belief systems.

Luckily, Brittany and Jeff had always talked openly about what was important to them. Although they felt they could talk safely and respectfully together, they had learned to use the Speaker-Listener Technique to help them discuss difficult issues. When they were ready to talk about core beliefs, they wanted to address the subject with additional structure. So they used their Speaker-Listener skills to communicate respectfully and fully, and faced the new issue as a team.

Over the course of several months, Brittany and Jeff met regularly to talk about beliefs and practices. It wasn't easy, but they made it a priority to talk about these parts of their relationship. They practiced talking respectfully and validated each other—showing they accepted each other's point of view even if they disagreed. Most important, they refused to let disagreements control them. They worked together to figure out how they could stay true to their own beliefs but be comfortable with how they would bring up their child.

To work out differences in worldviews, partners need two things:

1. An understanding of their own core beliefs—where they come from and why they're important. People who feel more secure in what they believe are less likely to be threatened by differences with their partner.
2. A commitment to talking safely and respectfully about differences in core beliefs. Each of you needs to make every effort to keep such differences from harming your marriage. The Speaker/Listener Technique can be helpful here.

The greater the differences couples have, the more important these conditions are. But whatever your differences, communicating clearly, being respectful, and, when needed, negotiating solutions will keep conflict from damaging your relationship.

When Conflict Interferes

Unlike Brittany and Jeff, Miriam and Andy didn't handle the differences in their beliefs well. In the beginning, everything was fine. The fact that he was Catholic and she was Jewish wasn't a problem for either of them. Neither was very religious, and they figured that if problems about belief systems came up in the future, they would just handle them then.

Andy's family and Miriam's family weren't as certain as the young couple. Both sets of parents had hoped that their children would marry someone of their own faith. They were concerned about how the couple would handle the problems they felt sure would come up. But when Andy and Miriam got engaged, all four parents decided not to press the issue. Both families were close, and none of the parents wanted to lose their children because of religious differences.

Soon after graduation, Andy and Miriam married. A judge presided at the wedding, and both sets of family members attended. But not long after Andy and Miriam came back from their honeymoon, Miriam's father died unexpectedly. Miriam was beside herself with grief. She had loved her father very deeply, and was shocked that he was no longer part of her life.

Andy jumped right in to help Miriam through her difficult time. He did everything he could for her, and she appreciated his thoughtfulness and sensitivity. Eventually the two got back to normal life, setting up their home and getting involved with careers and activities.

Soon it was pretty clear, though, that something had changed. Miriam began talking about Judaism. She began to wonder if she shouldn't become more involved in her faith.

The death of Miriam's father had a big effect on her feelings about religion. Something that hadn't been very important to her suddenly took on new significance. The fact that her father had been such a great man, and had been religious, made her think that being more religious might be a good thing.

When she brought all this up to Andy, his first reaction was unhappiness. Religion still wasn't very important to him, and he couldn't imagine making religious practice a big part of their lives. Then he wondered if Miriam would want to raise their children Jewish, which would leave him out of the picture. He also wondered if his parents would get even more upset about his marriage. He started to worry that Miriam's new interest in religion was going to be a big problem in lots of ways.

All Andy could see was trouble. So whenever Miriam brought the subject up, their conversation went something like this:

MIRIAM: Andy, I was thinking I'd go to the local temple this Friday night and see what the service was like. What do you think? Would you go with me?

ANDY: Honey, you know I'm just not interested in that kind of thing. Beside, that comedian we liked so much is playing again downtown. I thought we could catch him Friday night, and maybe get some dinner before the show.

MIRIAM: Well, we could go to see him on Saturday. I'd really like to go to the service on Friday. And it would be great if you would go with me.

> ANDY: *(getting annoyed)* Miriam, I just don't know what's gotten into you. You never used to care about religion. And I still don't. Can't we just have some fun on the weekends?
>
> MIRIAM: *(trying to stay calm)* It wouldn't take a lot of time. I think the services are only about an hour. Couldn't you try it with me once? I'd really like it if we went together.
>
> ANDY: *(very annoyed)* No, I'm not going to go to temple. You go if you want, but I sure don't understand why you want to. I'm going to stay home and watch TV and take it easy.
>
> MIRIAM: OK, OK, I guess I'll think some more about going by myself. Why don't we plan on going to see that comedian on Saturday?

Miriam quickly got the message that Andy didn't want to talk about her new interest, and decided it wasn't worth fighting over. But she also decided to start learning more about Judaism to see if it was right for her.

Now Miriam and Andy were not only not talking about an important issue. They started spending less time together, because Miriam joined several Jewish groups on her own. They also found that they argued more when they did do things together, and it began to feel like the fun was going out of their marriage. Their home was no longer the safe and happy place it had been.

Miriam and Andy buried the issue of religion because they were both afraid it would hurt their relationship. As it turned out, their marriage did suffer—not because of the issue—but because they didn't handle the issue well.

Dealing with the Issue

Things kept getting worse and worse for Andy and Miriam. Miriam got more involved with Jewish activities. Andy remained completely uninterested in any religious involvement. Neither wanted to change, and neither could talk about their feelings without getting upset.

Finally things got very bad. Both partners began to wonder if they were headed for divorce. Happily for them, a close friend recommended that they see a counselor. When they talked about the suggestion, they both quickly agreed. Despite their differences, they realized that they still loved each other. They hoped that seeing a counselor would help them stay together and find the happiness and closeness they had shared.

Happily again, the counselor they went to was encouraging and easy to be with. Both Miriam and Andy respected the woman and felt comfortable following her suggestions. One of the big things she taught them was the importance of talking about difficult issues, and how destructive it could be to bury them. She helped them learn the kinds of techniques we recommend throughout these 12 hours to talk about their religious differences in addition to continuing to meet with her.

Under the counselor's guidance, Andy and Miriam started to understand each other's concerns. They also discussed why religion had become important to Miriam and why it wasn't to Andy. Even though they continued to disagree on a lot of things, they were finally able to hear each other's point of view and bring up the subject calmly. By setting aside certain times to discuss the issue, they were also able to keep conflict from getting in the way of fun.

Miriam and Andy didn't turn things around overnight. It took a lot of time and work, and it wasn't easy. Eventually, though, they started to feel more confident that they would be able to find a solution. And by working on it together, they became closer and happier instead of drawing further apart.

Overcoming the Negatives of Interfaith Marriage

People today are far more likely than ever before to marry someone of a different religion. Our society is more mobile, which makes it easier to meet people with different backgrounds. In addition, our busy, complex lives can make it much harder to maintain a connection with a particular religious community.

Despite the upturn in mixed-faith marriages, research still shows that couples who practice different religions are more likely to divorce. If you're part of an interfaith marriage, it's important that you and your spouse understand that your risk is a bit higher.

But that doesn't mean you should worry that you can't beat the odds. And it doesn't mean that you shouldn't marry if you're now engaged or going together. Many mixed-faith couples have long and loving marriages. With respect, openness, and a thoughtful handling of differences, your team can safely and happily reach home plate.

For extra support and guidance, consider consulting a marriage counselor or a religious counselor, taking a class for interfaith couples, or reading books on the topic. We recommend *Mixed Matches: How to Create Successful Interracial, Interethnic and Interfaith Relationships,* by our colleague Joel Crohn; other books include *Celebrating Our Differences,* by Mary Helene Rosenbaum and Stanley Rosenbaum, or *The Interfaith Family Guidebook,* by Joan C. Hawxhurst (see her excellent Web site, www.dovetail.org).

TALKING ABOUT CORE BELIEFS

Whatever your core beliefs, they're an important part of what makes you *you*. They affect how you behave, how you relate to other people, how you raise your children, how you approach your life. In fact, they make a difference in nearly everything you do.

The same goes for your partner. But even if he or she was brought up in almost the exact same way you were, it's unlikely that your beliefs are exactly the same. Relationships, experiences, traditions, and culture all influence people to believe in different ways and honor different values.

It's pretty certain that you and your partner view the world at least somewhat differently. But whether the differences are big or small, you can protect your marriage by handling them well. That means doing several things:

- Talk about your beliefs, clearly, openly, and honestly.
- Negotiate and experiment with finding ways to live comfortably with your differences.
- Face your differences as a team.
- Back yourselves up with a religious or social support network.
- Discuss issues or differences before they trigger conflict.
- Agree to honor the four key values: commitment, intimacy, respect, and forgiveness.

⚡ POWER-UP EXERCISES

INDIVIDUAL EXERCISE

Take out your notebook and think and write about what in this hour has had the greatest impact on you.

COUPLE EXERCISE

The following questions will help you explore your core beliefs and values. The questions cover a broad range of issues, and you can answer them as they affect you religiously or philosophically.

After thinking about each question, you might want to write down your answers. This will help you to reflect on them further. And if you choose to share your answers, it will give your partner a clear idea of your thinking.

Next, if your partner is willing, plan several times to talk about your beliefs and feelings. Share your expectations about core beliefs, and talk about how reasonable you feel each other's expectations are. Discuss how you'll handle differences. Use the Speaker-Listener Technique if you need help keeping your discussions safe and respectful.

1. What is your worldview? In other words, what do you believe in?
2. How did you come to believe the way you do? What affected your point of view?

3. According to your belief system, what is the purpose of life?

4. What were your beliefs growing up? What religious or spiritual practices did you observe?

5. What does being spiritual mean to you? What does being religious mean?

6. According to your belief system, what is marriage?

7. If you're married, what vows did you make at your wedding? If you're planning to marry, what vows do you plan to make? Do these words tie into your belief system?

8. What is your feeling about divorce? Is the way you view it part of your belief system?

9. How do you honor (or expect to honor) your core beliefs in your relationship? (This includes religious beliefs, spiritual practices, philosophy, or something else.)

10. How does your belief system affect your day-to-day relationship?

11. Does your belief system include beliefs about sexuality? If so, what are those beliefs? How do they affect your relationship?

12. How does your belief system affect the way you raise, or expect to raise, your children?

13. Do you give money to a religious or other organization related to your belief system? How much do you give? If you're planning to marry, do you both agree to continue giving and to give the same amount?

14. Do you see any potential areas of conflict with your partner regarding your belief system? If you do, what are they?

15. What do you believe about forgiveness? How does it apply to your relationship with your partner?

16. What do you believe about being responsible to others?

17. What do you believe about respecting others? How should you and your partner show respect to each other?

18. How do you observe religious holidays? If you plan to marry, will you continue to observe them in the same way?

19. What is your belief about death? Do you believe in an afterlife? What is your belief about matters relating to the end of life, such as living wills and organ donation?

20. Are there other issues about your belief system that you would like to talk about with your partner?

PART III

ROUNDING THIRD

*H*ere you are at third base already! If you've been learning the skills and techniques we've suggested in the eight hours so far, you're on your way to more closeness, more fun, and more satisfaction in your relationship. Very soon you'll reach "home" by achieving a new level of happiness in what can truly be a great marriage.

What's up next? In this part of the 12-hour program, we're going to concentrate on expectations and forgiveness. We're going to show you how having realistic expectations and respecting those of your partner will increase feelings of closeness and satisfaction with your relationship. We'll also show you how being able to forgive will not only get you past the pain you'll inevitably cause each other over the years—even if your marriage is the happiest—but also help your love, intimacy, and joy to grow.

Parts One and Two have given you lots of ways to protect and preserve your love and marriage as you handle the curve balls life often throws at you. Here we're going to give you a way of handling problems you sometimes create on your own because of unrealistic expectations and the inability to forgive.

HOUR 9

Meeting Expectations

Just what are expectations? They're things we consider probable or certain—our beliefs about the way things will or should be. For example, you might expect a raise at work, think it likely that your child will forget to take her lunch again tomorrow, or figure that your husband will want to go out with you tonight. Expectations are involved in nearly every part of life, from chores to careers to money to sex.

In the last hour we talked about the importance of discussing your values and philosophy of life with your partner. We pointed out how sharing a worldview, or coexisting happily with different views, was a key to marital happiness. We also talked about the importance of engaging in meaningful activities together as well as spending time with people who support your marriage.

In this hour we'll take a look at the role your conscious and not-so-conscious expectations play in your relationship. We'll discuss how important it is to have reasonable expectations and to do your best to be aware of your expectations, express them clearly, and meet your partner's expectations. We'll also show you how to keep mismatched expectations from hurting your team and even how to embrace differences.

WHERE DO EXPECTATIONS COME FROM?

Expectations develop from the combination of your individual experiences. They were created in your past, but they affect your present and future. The three most influential are

1. The family you grew up in
2. The relationships you've had
3. Cultural factors, such as family traditions, your ethnic background, your religious background, and things like advertising and movies

Each of these influences is unique for every person.

Family-of-Origin Influences

Even though you probably didn't know it at the time, the family you grew up in had a lot to do with the expectations you have now. The behavior, the patterns, the words, the interactions—all were influences on your ideas of how things are supposed to be. Some of these influences came directly from your parents, sisters or brothers, or other relatives or caregivers. Some of them you noticed and absorbed on your own.

For example, holidays may have been a special time for your mother. At Thanksgiving, she may have always invited all your family members, plus anyone who didn't have a place to celebrate, to come to your house and share a huge meal. She would decorate the table, have chocolate turkeys for the children, and cook three different potato dishes so everyone would have the kind they liked. Every year she would tell you that Thanksgiving was her favorite holiday. She would also say that no one should ever spend a holiday alone. And every year you had a great time eating delicious food and playing with cousins, neighbors, and even kids you hadn't known.

Now you're an adult, and Thanksgiving isn't far away. And guess what? Very likely your idea of the perfect Thanksgiving is pretty much like your mother's. You expect that you and your spouse will invite a big group of people for dinner, include the elderly widower down the street, and serve three different potato dishes.

The same kind of thing goes for relationships. For instance, if you saw your parents hugging and kissing a lot, you may very well expect that you and your spouse will express affection openly. If arguing and fighting was the way your folks faced problems, it's likely you think that's the way disagreements are handled. If your older sister made sure no one picked on you at school, you probably expect that your older child will look out for the younger. Here's an example of how these kinds of expectations can play out in a marriage.

Antoine and Latoya grew up in very different households. Antoine's parents divorced when he was young, and Antoine was raised by his mother. She was a very strong woman, and handled everything well. She had a full-time job as an insurance agent, took care of the house, and made sure that Antoine got a great education.

Latoya came from a two-parent family. But in her family, her father was very much in charge. He had been brought up in a home where his mom took care of the kids and his dad made the big decisions—about how money would be spent, what proper behavior was, and so on. So his own home worked the same way. Latoya's mother was responsible for the day-to-day care of Latoya and her brothers and sisters. Latoya's father was away on business a lot, but still made most of the important decisions for the family.

The difference in Latoya's and Antoine's backgrounds made for differences in their expectations, which caused problems when it came time to make their own decisions. Antoine expected that Latoya would have a lot to say about an issue. But Latoya assumed that Antoine would take responsibility to make the decisions for both of them.

The problem came to a head when Antoine's mother had a bad fall. After surgery on her hip, she needed care and physical therapy for several weeks. Antoine wondered if he and Latoya should have his mom recuperate at their home. On the one hand, their house was small, and it would mean that both he and Latoya would have to give up some of their regular activities. On the other hand, it would be expensive to have his mom go to a rehabilitation home or to have an aide come to her apartment.

Antoine wanted to talk it over with Latoya. But she said that whatever he decided would be OK with her.

Once again all the responsibility was on Antoine's shoulders. This time it was too much for him, and he decided they had to make a change. He had read about communication strategies and the PREP approach on the Web. He asked Latoya to discuss the problem with him following those safe strategies.

Here's some of what they said.

ANTOINE: You know, since we've been married, it seems I make almost all the big decisions. Everything from what kind of insurance we should have to how much we should put into savings. It's gotten really hard for me, having all the responsibility.

LATOYA: You feel like it's too much to do on your own.

ANTOINE: Yeah. My mom always made the decisions because my dad wasn't around. She did it, but I saw how hard it was for her to make them alone. So I always thought we'd make family decisions together. But you don't seem to want to.

LATOYA: Well, my mom never made any of the important family decisions. My dad always set the rules. So I guess I just thought you would handle the big stuff.

ANTOINE: When you were growing up, your dad made all the important decisions. So you thought that's the way it should be done.

LATOYA: I never really thought about it before, but I guess I just assumed you would want to make the big decisions because my dad did. But it sounds like you're not happy that way. That you'd rather have us do it together.

ANTOINE: Definitely. It's too much responsibility on my own. But at least now I understand why you've hung back from making decisions. Do you want to talk about how we can work on that? Then, later on, I'd like to talk with you about the best thing to do for my mom.

Once they realized they had different expectations because of differing backgrounds, and had a good discussion about their expectations, Antoine and Latoya had a much easier time dealing with decisions. Antoine encouraged Latoya to talk about issues and help make choices. The more she got involved, the more confident she became. The more they made decisions as a team, the easier Antoine slept at night.

Even if you and your partner grew up under similar circumstances, it's very possible that you have different expectations in a number of areas. It's also possible that you have similar expectations though you come from very different backgrounds. It's likely that you'll have some of the same expectations and differ in others. What's important is that you take the time to understand your expectations and share them with your partner.

Influences from Previous Relationships

Just as the way your early home life affects how you are now, your earlier relationships shape the expectations you have for your current relationship. This is especially true for previous romantic relationships. From those relationships you develop expectations about the kind of kissing and lovemaking your partner will like, how you'll spend time together, how you'll discuss—or not discuss—problems, who should make the first move, what's off-limits, how commitment is shown, and how he or she likes to be romanced.

For instance, say that as a teenager you got in trouble with the police. It happened only once, and you definitely learned your lesson. When you decided to share that part of your history with a previous partner during a very intimate discussion, the talk seemed to go well. But a few days later you broke up, and you were sure that what you told her was the reason. The experience made you feel that you could never mention it again. You developed the expectation that if you revealed this part of yourself to someone you loved, he or she would think you were a horrible person and never see you again.

Now, in your current relationship, you've kept back the information. But doing that turns out not to be a good thing. As we discussed earlier, an important part of a strong relationship is being able to share everything, even those things that make you feel vulnerable. If you don't reveal your mistake and your turnaround to your partner, it can prevent you from reaching a deep level of intimacy.

Keeping back important information can also show that you don't trust your partner to know the real you. If you were hurt when you revealed yourself before, it's understandable that you wouldn't want to do it again. But studies show that people who expect others to be untrustworthy have more problems in their relationships.

Expectations based on previous relationships affect day-to-day situations as well as bigger issues. For example, Melissa and Paul didn't agree on who should fill Melissa's car with gas. Paul had been married before, and his first wife had been pretty traditional. When they were dating, she had always expected Paul to ask her out and to pay for whatever they did on their dates. When they were married, she had expected Paul to open doors for her, fill her car with gas, take out the garbage, and give her order to the waiter when they went out to eat.

Now Paul is with Melissa, and she is very different from his first wife. She's much less traditional. She also has lived on her own for some time and is used to doing everything for herself. When Paul does the things his first wife had expected—fills Melissa's car with gas, takes her arm crossing the street—Melissa thinks that Paul thinks she's weak or unable to take of herself. She gets very annoyed, which always surprises Paul. He thinks he's doing things that should make Melissa happy.

After some self-reflection based on the quiz on page 193, and after talking safely as teammates, Paul and Melissa discovered that their problems were based on expectations from previous relationships. By discussing them, they got to the heart of the matter. Melissa was able to tell Paul that his actions made her feel incapable. He told her that his previous wife had liked them, so he had expected Melissa would too. By learning what did please Melissa, Paul was able to adjust his actions. And Melissa learned that Paul wasn't trying to make her dependent, but rather that he loved her and was trying to make her happy.

Expectations and Negative Interpretations

When your partner doesn't meet your expectations, you may start wondering why. Be on guard for negative interpretations if you do that. When an expectation isn't met, you can develop a new negative expectation, such as believing that your partner isn't meeting your needs on purpose or that he or she doesn't care.

In Paul and Melissa's case, Paul quickly understood that Melissa liked to do things for herself. But what if it took him a while to change his ways, because he was so used to doing what his first wife had liked? Melissa might start to believe that he doesn't care enough about her to do the things that are important to her. Then minor things like holding open a door could lead to major conflict.

The only way to address these kinds of negative interpretations is to talk openly with your partner about your concerns and your expectations.

Cultural Influences

A variety of cultural factors influence expectations. These include everything from the TV shows you watch to your religious upbringing to your ethnic background. They all can have a powerful effect on your relationship.

For example, you may have grown up in a family whose culture encourages arranged marriages. Your spouse may have been chosen for you, and you may have met only a short time before you were married. If that was the case for you, you probably expect that you'll arrange your own son or daughter's marriage. You expect that the tradition will continue.

Or maybe you grew up in a family which expected that all members would celebrate every special occasion together. Doing something other than being with your relatives for a family celebration wasn't an option for you. Now, as an adult, you might be surprised when your spouse sees nothing wrong with letting your teenager celebrate her birthday with her friends instead of her family.

Societal influences—TV shows, advertising, magazines, and the like—also greatly affect expectations. If a popular TV show depicts couples living together outside of marriage, you may decide that it's OK, even though you were brought up to believe it wasn't. Or if a commercial shows a cheerful mom working outside the home, raising two children, and keeping a spotless house, you may come to believe that all women should be able to happily do the same.

Cultural and ethnic influences can be reflected in the choices we make about expressing our native culture and lifestyle. They can also affect more basic life choices, such as your ideas about appropriate marriage partners and how to raise children.

RELATIONSHIP QUIZ

Begin this quiz by thinking about each of the following parts of your life:

- The family you grew up in
- The relationships you've had
- Cultural factors that influence you—your ethnicity, family traditions, and so on

Now answer the following questions as they relate to each of the three areas.

1. Are there any similarities or differences between the way this area affected your past relationships and how it affects your current relationship?
2. Are the similarities or differences a source of conflict in your current relationship?
3. How do you feel when the differences come up in your current relationship? Are you disappointed, hurt, angry, confused, or something else? Why do you think you feel this way?
4. Do you and your partner ever talk about the feelings brought up by these similarities or differences? If you do, are your discussions constructive, and do they lead to

---

mutual understanding? Or are they destructive, distancing you or leading to more conflict (or both)? Why do you think the discussions end the way they do?

HOW EXPECTATIONS AFFECT RELATIONSHIPS

As you've seen, expectations are often involved in big issues as well as small ones. Because they come into play so often, it probably won't surprise you that they're a key part of marital happiness. If you expect something to happen and it doesn't, you may become sad, disappointed, or angry. Often you see this connection between expectations and your relationship when events trigger conflict around issues. You get into a conflict because your unmet expectations can lead to strong negative feelings.

Bruce and Cindy discovered they had very different expectations when their last child left for college. Money had always been tight, so Bruce assumed Cindy would go back to working full-time. Cindy was used to working two days a week and wanted to use her newfound free time for exercise, volunteer work, and other things she'd never had the time for before the kids were gone. When the issue came up, Cindy and Bruce found themselves in a major disagreement.

BRUCE: I'm really shocked that you don't want to go back to work full-time. I just assumed you would. We need the extra money for the kids' schools. And I'd sure like not to feel so strapped all the time.

CINDY: Both of the kids have scholarships. And we've done OK so far. I've really been looking forward to having some time for myself. I feel like I've been working plus cooking and cleaning and driving kids to activities and solving squabbles forever. I need to take a break.

> BRUCE: *(upset)* Well, I'd like to take a break too. But you don't see me working part-time. I thought you'd want to help out the family as much as you could. I guess you don't care that much about me and our life together now that the kids aren't around any more.
>
> CINDY: *(very angry)* I can't believe you said that. Of course I care about you and our family. I just need a little bit of time to myself.
>
> BRUCE: *(heading for the door)* Well, I think you're being incredibly selfish. I'm not going to talk to you when you're acting this way.

Bruce had expected that Cindy thought the same way he did. Cindy assumed that Bruce would understand how she felt. But because they hadn't talked about the issue, their differing expectations erupted into a fight. Neither expectation was unreasonable. But when they collided, conflict claimed the day.

Part of the couple's conflict had to do with hidden issues. The surface issue was disagreement over family priorities now that the kids were in college—no small matter. But their argument also showed that Cindy felt she was being stifled and controlled.

Like Bruce and Cindy, many couples have different expectations, sometimes with hidden issues buried beneath. This can cause great unhappiness. But by airing and handling the differences and issues, you can prevent unhappiness and strengthen your bond. Here's how to do it.

MANAGING EXPECTATIONS

Four factors are key to managing your expectations:

1. *Being aware* of what you expect
2. *Being reasonable* about what you expect
3. *Being clear* about what you expect

4. *Being motivated* to meet your partner's expectations, even when they're different from your own

Being Aware of What You Expect

It may sound crazy, but we're often not even aware of a lot of the things we expect. For example, when Sunday nights roll around, you might feel slightly disappointed if your whole family doesn't spend the evening together. You don't know exactly why, but somehow you wish everyone were there.

Then you take a minute to think about it. And, bingo, you know why you're slightly sad. When you were a child, Sunday evenings were family time. Everyone got together for a meal of leftovers. Then you played cards or a board game and had a great time relaxing together.

The disappointment you feel now comes from subconsciously expecting that your own family would spend Sunday nights together too.

Feeling disappointed is a telltale sign that you had an expectation that wasn't met. When you feel disappointed or sad, stop for a minute and think about what happened. What were you expecting? Did you know you were expecting it? Was it reasonable to expect it would happen?

The exercises at the end of this hour will help you and your partner become more aware of your expectations. They will also help you understand how reasonable they are and show you how to share them. Understanding your expectations and talking about how you want things to be will help you shape your vision of your future together and help bring you closer.

Being Reasonable About What You Expect

In addition to bringing hidden expectations to their marriage, partners also may bring unreasonable expectations. One of the biggest is that their new partner will meet all their needs.

This just isn't possible. Even the most loving and well-matched couples will disagree, have different expectations, and let each other down from time to time. It's not realistic or even appropriate to think that our marriage partner will satisfy all the conscious and subconscious needs and issues we carry with us from our childhood, family of origin, previous relationships, and workplace.

Pursuing unreasonable expectations is likely to lead to conflict, because those kinds of expectations just can't be met. So it's incredibly important to separate reasonable expectations from unreasonable ones.

Rajesh and Sangeeta were having trouble handling their differences. After using the techniques recommended in the earlier parts of this book, they began to make real progress. They discussed important issues using the Speaker-Listener Technique. And they made it a rule that they would keep conflict out of their fun times together.

Although their relationship definitely improved, Sangeeta thought it wasn't enough. Her expectation was that once they used their new skills, disagreements would completely disappear.

This was an unreasonable expectation. Using the skills and principles of our approach helps most couples protect and preserve their love. But nothing will stop all conflict.

Sangeeta's unreasonable expectation prevented her from realizing how far she and Rajesh had come. It also made Rajesh feel unappreciated. He had put a lot of effort into handling their conflicts, and felt they had made a lot of progress. Sangeeta's unhappiness made him wonder if things were hopeless.

Having an expectation doesn't always mean it's a reasonable one. To help you distinguish reasonable expectations from unreasonable ones, take some time to do the exercise at the end of this chapter. Evaluate each expectation you have with your partner. Then work as a team to adjust unreasonable expectations or agree to let them go because they can't be met.

Being Clear About What You Expect

Some expectations you have may be perfectly reasonable. But if they're not expressed, they probably won't be met.

For instance, Teri is quite shy, but her fiancé Carl is very outgoing. Because Carl is a manager for his company, he's expected to attend a lot of company dinners and other functions. Teri always goes with him. But she usually has a pretty bad time. While Carl talks to customers and colleagues, Teri either stands with him smiling or is all on her own. She doesn't know much about Carl's business, and feels that she has nothing in common with the people at the parties.

Whenever they go to a business event, Teri hopes Carl will stay with her and steer conversations to something she can talk about. But because she has never said that she'd like this to happen, it never does. Teri knows Carl loves her and wants her to be happy. So she expects he'll realize that she's uncomfortable and do what he can to help her out. Carl thinks Teri is bright and charming, and just assumes she'll be fine meeting new people.

If you don't make your expectations clear to your partner, most likely they won't be met. Once you and your partner have pinpointed your expectations through the exercise at the end of the chapter, talk about them openly. Sharing your perspectives will help you share a long and happy marriage.

Being Motivated to Meet Your Partner's Expectations

One of the biggest reasons most relationships start out well is that both partners are motivated to make each other happy. You try to figure out what your partner likes and wants and then try to make it happen.

Later on, though, meeting your partner's expectations can become less important, especially if the expectations are different from your own. But continuing to meet reasonable expectations is very important to your marriage. Doing something to please your partner is going to make him or her happy. And isn't that something teammates want to do?

Decide right now to put some positive energy into meeting one of your partner's expectations. If you generally don't like skiing but your husband always wishes you did, go with him once and take a lesson. If your wife wishes you'd share her interest in religion, accompany her to a service. (If you're not sure what to focus on, plan to meet one of the expectations you discuss during the Power-Up Exercises on pages 200–203.) Try to meet an expectation for no other reason than because it will bring your partner happiness. You'll probably find that it makes you happy too.

More Research About Expectations

Researchers at the University of Maryland and the University of North Carolina at Chapel Hill discovered that expectations often focus on three major areas:

1. *Boundaries:* For example, how much independence is OK for each partner? What kinds of relationships with other people are acceptable?
2. *Investment:* For example, how much time and effort does each partner think the other should be putting into the relationship? Are both partners planning to have the relationship last their whole lives?
3. *Control and power:* For example, who will make particular decisions? Will power be shared, and if so, how?

These researchers have also discovered that it's not crucial that partners have the same expectations to be happy. Instead, it's more important that partners try to meet each other's most important and realistic wishes.

ACCEPTING THE FACT THAT SOME REASONABLE EXPECTATIONS WON'T BE MET

If you're like most people, you probably have a number of things you want to have happen in your marriage. Some are very important expectations, and some not so critical. But even if they're all reasonable, it's unlikely they'll all come true. When something you want is realistic and you've made your desire clear to your spouse, it can be very painful to learn that it simply will never happen.

For example, if your partner is a police officer, you may be worried about the danger and wish he would choose a different career. It's a reasonable expectation, because you love him and want him to be safe. But if he loves his work, he's probably not going to change jobs.

Then you can either get angry and sulk, or you can accept the fact, learn to live with it, and move on. Certainly you can grieve the loss of your expectation, and you should acknowledge the disappointment and pain. But you also need to put it in perspective. When you commit to one person, you commit to who that person is. If your expectation falls outside those bounds, then you need to understand that it's not going to happen.

Our advice is to work together as hard as you can to meet each other's expectations. When you discover that some of the reasonable expectations won't be met, keep working together to manage the disappointment. Be open about each issue. For example, your partner might say, "I know you wish I had a different career. I know you don't like to worry, and I don't want you to. But this is the career that makes me happy and lets me help a lot of other people."

Enjoying the good things about your marriage will help you stay close. Facing the hard things together will too. In fact, the most amazing marriages we've seen are those in which the partners join together in accepting disappointment and by doing so become even closer.

⚡ POWER-UP EXERCISES

INDIVIDUAL EXERCISE

Take out your notebook and think and write about what in this chapter had the greatest effect on you.

COUPLE EXERCISE

This exercise has three parts. Part 1 asks you to explore your expectations. If you and your partner want to do the exercise together, first write your answers down individually, then share them in a safe and respectful way. Take plenty of time to think about the questions in light of how you want your relationship to be, not how it is. Be sure to say what you really think, even if it's a little embarrassing.

Part 2 asks you to rate your expectations according to how reasonable they are. You'll use a rating system from 1 to 10 and note any expectations you've never discussed.

Part 3 encourages you to talk about your expectations together and how they affect your future.

PART 1

What are your expectations about?

1. *How long your relationship will last.* Is it "till death do us part?"
2. *Love.* Do you expect you'll love each other forever? What would keep that from happening? What is the most important way you show your love? What shows you that you're loved?
3. *Your sexual relationship.* How often will you make love? What kinds of things are OK? What's off-limits?
4. *Sexual and emotional fidelity.* Will you stay faithful to your mate and expect the same?
5. *Romance.* What kinds of things are romantic to you?
6. *Children.* Do you want to have children (or more children)? How many?
7. *Children from a previous relationship.* If you or your partner has children from another relationship, where will they live? How will you share in their upbringing?
8. *Work and income.* Will both of you work, now and in the future? Is one job more important? If you have children or plan to, will one or both of you stop working or work part-time?

9. *Emotional dependency.* Do you want to be taken care of? Do you want to take care of your partner? How much will you rely on each other to get through difficult times?

10. *Your approach to life.* Do you think of yourselves as a team? Or do you think you're two independent individuals?

11. *Loyalty.* What is your definition of the term?

12. *Communicating about problems.* Will you talk about problems or avoid them until you have to face them? If you talk about them, how will you do it?

13. *Power and control.* Who do you expect to have more power? In making all decisions or just some? For example, who will control the money? Who will care for the children? How do you feel about sharing power or giving it up?

14. *Household tasks.* Who do you expect will do what around the house? How much household work will each of you do?

15. *Religious beliefs and practices.* How, when, and where do you expect to practice your faith if you're religious? If you have different religious beliefs, cultural backgrounds, or family traditions, how will you work them out? How will they affect your relationship?

16. *Time together.* How much time do you expect to spend together? How much with friends, at work, with family, or alone? Is it acceptable to you to spend time apart?

17. *Sharing feelings.* Do you expect to share all your feelings? Should some things be kept private?

18. *Being friends.* What is your definition of a friend? Do you expect to be your partner's friend?

19. *Everyday things.* What are the little things that irritate you or might irritate you? For example, should the toilet seat be left up or down? Who should hold the remote control? What should you do if one of you snores? Is it necessary to send thank-you notes when you receive a gift?

20. *Forgiveness.* How important is forgiveness in your relationship?

21. *Other relationships.* What other relationships are OK for both of you to have? Friendships with people of the opposite sex? Friendships with coworkers? When you're not together, how much time is OK to spend with other people?

22. *Other important issues.* Write down how you feel about any issue not covered in the list.

Once you've answered all the questions, think about the hidden issues discussed in Hour 3: power, caring, recognition, commitment, integrity, and acceptance. Do you see particular ways these issues influence or are influenced by your expectations? For example, could a power issue affect who holds the remote control when you watch TV?

PART 2

Now, on a scale of 1 to 10, rate how reasonable you think each expectation is. A completely reasonable expectation would be a 10, a completely unreasonable expectation a 1. After you rate your expectations, put a check mark next to any that you and your partner have never thoroughly discussed.

PART 3

After you both complete Parts 1 and 2, start talking about your expectations. Plan several times for discussions, covering just one or two expectations each time. You may want to use the Speaker-Listener Technique to keep your talks structured and safe.

As you talk, cover these areas:

- The degree to which each of you feels the expectation was made clear in the past
- The degree to which each of you feels the expectation is reasonable or unreasonable
- What you should do about unreasonable expectations
- Your long-term vision for your relationship
- Your expectations about your future together

HOUR 10

Forgiving

EXPECTATIONS WERE THE TOPIC OF HOUR 9. You learned how strongly these "should be's" affect your relationship. And you learned how important it is to be aware of your expectations, to be realistic and clear about them, and also to try hard to make your partner's expectations come true. Doing all those things will help you both take a giant step toward home plate.

You also learned in Hour 9 that even in the best of all possible relationships, some of your expectations just aren't going to be met, even if they make lots of sense and are very important to you; that the best thing you can do is accept the disappointment, learn to live with it, and move on.

Expectations aren't the only things in marriage—even in a great marriage—that won't always go the way you want them to. When two people spend a great deal of time together, it's inevitable that one will do something that makes the other unhappy. Being in a relationship makes it possible for you to experience extraordinary joy and have an exciting and fulfilling life. But it can also leave you open to pain and sadness.

If you've been in a relationship for even a short time, it's likely you've already been hurt in some way. The pain might have come from something major, such as finding out that your partner didn't tell you the truth about how that dent got in the car. Or it might have come from something much smaller, such as having your partner say something insensitive about the way you look when you get up in the morning.

It's also likely that you've done some hurting yourself, through either your actions or inactions. We all make mistakes. But whoever did what to whom, the person who was hurt probably felt somewhere between pretty bad and downright awful. When you're hurt, it's also possible to feel that you'll never be able to forgive your partner for what happened.

Research shows that many marriages are destroyed by the resentment that builds up when partners hurt each other. But it also shows that some couples are able to get beyond the pain—from put-downs, affairs, forgetfulness, bad decisions, negative interpretations, abusive comments, rudeness, thoughtlessness, and the other harmful things partners do—and find happiness on the other side.

How is this possible? We think it's because those couples have learned how to forgive. In this hour we're going to show you how critical forgiveness is in maintaining your bond, and how powerful an expression it is of your love and commitment. We're going to look at responsibility and trust, two important parts of forgiveness. And we're going to give you specific steps for working through a difficult issue by incorporating forgiveness as part of the healing process.

Our work has shown that to be the best partner you can be, you need to take responsibility for your actions, ask for forgiveness, and forgive your partner for his or her actions or inactions. Forgiveness is as much about forgiving your partner as it is about his or her forgiving you. Only when you both can face the person you've hurt can the emotional or physical pain that's been caused be resolved. And then the healing can begin.

WHAT IS FORGIVENESS?

The dictionary tells us that to forgive is to "grant pardon for an offense or a sin," "to cancel," "to cease to feel resentment against." We agree it's all of that, but it is also

- Giving up the urge (or what you may think is your right) to get even
- A choice you have to make
- A process that takes time

Forgiving is much more than saying, "I forgive you." And it can sometimes take a lot longer to do than it takes to say the words. To us, forgiving is not only pardoning your partner for hurting you, without taking revenge, but also helping your partner out of the doghouse.

When your partner does something wrong that hurts you, in your mind you send him or her straight to the doghouse. Not forgiving keeps your partner there and makes it impossible for you to move forward as a team. When you don't work as a team, intimacy, love, and real happiness stay out of reach.

When you forgive, you need to do more than say the words and mean them. You also have to extend a forgiving, helping hand. To truly forgive, you need to be gracious to your partner. Being kind and generous as well as granting pardon will put you back on the same footing and keep your love strong.

Forgiveness Gives Hope

If you don't forgive your partner, it's possible that hopelessness will set in for one or both of you. That's because you will keep sending messages that say "I will never forgive you." For example, you might speak or act in a way that communicates the following messages:

"I'm going to hold this against you forever."

"I'm going to get even for what you did to me."

"You're going to pay for this big time."

"You're never going to live this down."

If you say things like this often (to yourself or to your partner), you'll probably start acting in ways that make them come true. Then, after a while, your partner will think that no matter what he or she does, you will never forgive him or her—that's a recipe for hopelessness. Moreover, if he or she believes there's no hope for redemption, it's possible your partner will walk away.

Forgiving means that you're not going to keep score or keep reminding your partner that you've got the upper hand. Scorekeeping only leads to resentment and finally to a lack of hope. Forgiveness means throwing away the scorecard and inviting your partner back onto the field.

WHAT FORGIVENESS IS NOT

OK, now you've got a pretty good idea of what we mean by forgiving. But you may still have in your mind that old expression "forgive and forget."

To us, forgiving has nothing to do with forgetting. Just think of something really painful that was done to you in the past. Have you forgiven the person who did it? We hope you have. Have you forgotten what took place? Probably not. Something that brought you pain, disappointment, or sadness is unlikely to disappear completely from your mind. To forgive doesn't mean you have to forget.

Forgiving also doesn't mean several other things:

- It doesn't mean you won't feel any more pain.
- It doesn't mean the person who hurt you shouldn't take responsibility for his or her actions.

- It doesn't mean you have to be friends with the person you forgive.

Even when you've completely forgiven your partner, you may still feel pain from what he or she did. Some people think this means you really haven't forgiven. But that's not so. The pain you feel is actually grief over the loss of trust or the deceit or whatever it was that happened, and it may continue for some time.

Forgiving also doesn't mean the person who hurt you shouldn't take responsibility. When you say "I forgive you," you're not saying "You didn't do anything wrong." You're saying "I pardon you, and I won't hold it against you." Ideally your partner takes responsibility for his or her behavior and understands that it hurt you. When that happens, it makes it much easier for the two of you to move on. (You'll find more on responsibility on page 213.)

Finally, forgiving someone doesn't mean that you immediately have to be the best of friends. In extreme cases, you can forgive but not want to be close to the person until a destructive pattern has been changed. For example, your partner's alcohol abuse may have caused enormous damage to your relationship. If he says he has finally realized he's got to stop drinking, and has entered a rehabilitation program, you may decide to forgive him for the pain he has caused. But you may want to wait to see what happens before you reconcile. If he stops drinking and continues to go to counseling, then you may be willing to get back together.

BIG AND SMALL HURTS

When you think about being hurt, you might immediately think of the big things: your partner having an affair, abuse of you or your children, lying, cheating, or doing something else enormously wrong. But pain can result from everyday acts as well: forgetting an important appointment, saying something thoughtless, breaking a treasured object by mistake. How hurt you or your partner feels and how much damage is caused usually depend on how badly trust was violated.

Let's take a look at how the violation of trust affected two couples.

Dave and Melanie were engaged to be married, and both had been eager to make all the wedding arrangements together. But on the day they were to meet the caterer, only Melanie showed up. She was a teacher, and had left school the minute classes were over to make the appointment. Dave was supposed to leave work right after his last sales call.

When Dave didn't appear, Melanie met with the caterer and talked about possible menus. But because Dave didn't come, she had to make another appointment for him to taste the food as well. That meant taking more time away from schoolwork, but she didn't want to make the decisions without Dave.

When Dave saw Melanie that night, this is what happened.

MELANIE: *(upset)* Where were you this afternoon, Dave?

DAVE: What do you mean? I was at work. What . . . oh, no, I forgot the appointment with the caterer!

MELANIE: You did. It was so embarrassing. Plus I had to make another appointment, and she didn't have an opening for three weeks. It's going to put everything behind.

DAVE: Honey, I'm so sorry. It just went right out of my mind. I made a big sale today, and that's all I could think about.

MELANIE: Well, I'm glad about your sale. But we agreed we would do all the wedding stuff together. Then the first thing comes up and you don't show. I thought I could count on you. It feels like this isn't important to you.

DAVE: You're absolutely right, I should have been there. And it truly is important to me, please believe me. I'm really, really sorry. I promise I'll make it to all the other appointments. Can you forgive me?

Another couple, Mai and Trang, experienced much more pain from their conflict. Mai ran a consulting business out of their home, and spent a lot of time on the computer. Trang began to notice that she was on the Internet a lot at night too. When he asked her about it, she said she was doing research. But he also noticed that she was becoming more and more distant.

Finally he became suspicious that something was going on. Then he found an e-mail that Mai had printed out from a man he didn't know. The e-mail was very personal. It looked like Mai was having an affair.

When Trang confronted her about it, this is what happened.

TRANG: *(very upset)* Mai, I went into your office to get some paper clips before. I found this e-mail on your desk. Who is this man? Are you having an affair?

MAI: *(snatching away the e-mail)* Of course not. I wouldn't do that.

TRANG: *(still angry)* Then what does this mean? What's been going on?

MAI: It's nothing. I'm just . . . it's that . . . *(She burst into tears.)*

TRANG: You are having an affair! I knew it! How could you?

MAI: *(still crying)* I'm so sorry. I didn't mean it to happen. A friend referred him to me as a client. We e-mailed a lot because he lives out of town, and we really hit it off. I was feeling a little bored—we haven't exactly been getting along, you know—and I guess I flirted with him. It seemed pretty innocent. But then he asked if we could get together.

TRANG: *(yelling)* You met with him? I can't believe it! Did you sleep with him?

MAI: *(crying harder)* I'm so sorry. I don't know how it happened. And it was only once. As soon as I realized what I'd done, I broke it off. I'm never going to see him again. I love you. Can you ever forgive me?

On the grand scale of things, Mai's betrayal was definitely worse than Dave's forgetfulness. That's because Trang's trust was violated to a much greater extent than Melanie's was. But both Trang and Melanie were hurt by their mate's behavior. And both needed to decide if they could forgive what had happened.

Would you forgive Dave? What about Mai? Dave's forgetfulness was an oversight in the midst of an exciting event. Most likely you think Melanie should forgive him, especially because he apologized and took responsibility. He hurt Melanie, but not enormously.

Mai might be harder to forgive. She betrayed Trang's trust completely. Although she also took responsibility and apologized, the pain and damage she caused were great. But if she really loves Trang and he loves her, and if they both want their marriage to go on, forgiveness is possible. No matter how big the hurt, partners can eventually forgive each other and move forward together.

Not Forgiving Can Hurt Your Health

Being unable to forgive doesn't only damage your relationship. It can also damage your emotional and physical health. Research and clinical experience have shown that hanging on to resentment and bitterness can put you at risk for such conditions as depression, ulcers, high blood pressure, and rage. It can also put you at increased risk for divorce: we've seen many marriages dissolve as a result of long-held resentment.

Whether or not you both agree about what happened, you can still choose to forgive and move on. You'll prevent further damage to your marriage. And you'll protect your health and well-being.

TAKING RESPONSIBILITY

One of the major ways you can work toward forgiveness is to take responsibility for what you've done. As we said before, this doesn't mean that what you did was right. It means that you accept the fact that you did what you did. Taking responsibility shows your love and commitment. It also shows that you're willing to take the consequences for whatever you do.

That doesn't give your partner license to punish you. But if you've caused pain, you need to accept what you did and to do whatever you can to repair it. You need to let your partner know that you want to make amends and make things right. You also need to say that you're willing to take part in the work of healing.

Taking responsibility can be hard, especially if you've really wounded your partner. It may take humility, sacrifice, and more pain. But if you take responsibility willingly and well, you'll do a lot to make sure that what you did doesn't happen again. It will also give your partner hope that your love will go on. And it may even strengthen your relationship and make your partner respect you more.

Five Steps to Taking Responsibility

If you've wronged your partner in some way, it's up to him or her to forgive you. But you can help make that happen by taking responsibility for your own actions. Doing your part is all you can do. But by doing it thoughtfully and in a smart way, you'll increase the chances that your partner will do his or her part too. Here's how to take responsibility:

1. State clearly what you did.

2. Apologize and really mean it.

3. Accept the fact that your behavior was hurtful, even if you have to push yourself.

4. Take steps to make sure that you don't hurt your mate in that way again. This may involve changing certain behaviors or breaking a pattern that's causing problems.

5. Remember that your relationship is most important. If you don't want to take responsibility for your hurtful action, and even if you feel justified for behaving the way you did, you still need to take responsibility for the sake of your marriage.

Resolving Problems When Partners Take Responsibility and When They Won't

Let's take another look at Dave and Melanie. His forgetting the appointment with their caterer made Melanie wonder if she could count on him and if the wedding was as important to him as his work. But she realized it was just a mistake when Dave explained what had happened and apologized. He told Melanie that marrying her was the most important thing to him. He also promised he would be at all the other meetings, making Melanie feel that his missing the first appointment didn't mean he wasn't committed to her. He did everything he could to ease Melanie's fears.

The hurt Dave caused wasn't grave, and he took responsibility for screwing up. Melanie found the courage to forgive him, and she did. She felt a little nervous each time a wedding-related meeting came up. But Dave came through every time, and Melanie didn't hold the missed appointment against him.

But what should you do if your partner wrongs you in some way and won't take responsibility? Do you allow the relationship to continue as before? As you think about it, you need to be open to the possibility that your partner didn't intend to do anything wrong. For example, Dave didn't set out to miss the appointment. He didn't say, "Oh, well, Melanie can take care or it, I don't have to be there." He simply forgot because something else very exciting happened that distracted him, however wrongfully.

Often there can be a difference of opinion about the event that caused the problem. For example, Melanie worried that Dave's missing the meeting was a sign that he didn't really want to marry her. This hidden issue of commitment is part of Melanie's personal concerns, and it isn't up to Dave to take responsibility for Melanie's negative interpretation of what his forgetting meant. On that score, Melanie will have to push herself to take a more trusting and less negative view of what Dave actually did.

Trang and Mai weren't able to solve their problem easily. Trang felt unable to forgive Mai because she had hurt him so deeply. Although she asked to be forgiven, she refused to take all the responsibility for putting their marriage at risk. She explained that the only reason she had started up with the other man was because Trang had seemed to have lost interest in her. She was sorry she had hurt him, but she thought Trang had to share in the responsibility.

Trang believed everything was Mai's fault, and asked her to move out of the house. She did, but she kept calling Trang to apologize and to say how much she loved him and wanted to stay married.

Finally Trang agreed to meet with her. Mai apologized again and asked what she could do to make things better. Rather than continue to include Trang in the blame, she focused on what she had done and what she thought might help now. This made Trang less defensive and made him feel there was some reason to hope.

When an affair has taken place, two things relating to responsibility are often true. For many (but not all) couples, distance has usually grown in their marriage, making it more likely that an affair could happen. Both Trang and Mai had allowed distance to grow, so both were responsible in some way for that happening. But it's still Mai—the one who had the affair—who is totally responsible for violating trust and failing to protect the marriage. It's Mai, not Trang, who is responsible for allowing herself to get involved in another relationship. Making responsibility clear can help couples move forward.

Eventually Trang and Mai were able to talk about some of the reasons the two had become distant. A major issue was that Mai felt Trang spent too many evenings working. They didn't share time together the way they used to, so she had started spending her evenings at the computer. It turned out that Trang had been working more because his business wasn't doing well, but he hadn't told Mai because he didn't want to worry her. Getting things out in the open in a safe way made them both feel better.

Trang, though, was still hurt and angry. But underneath it all he knew he still loved Mai. He told her he thought he could forgive her, but they would need to make some changes. Mai immediately started looking for a marriage counselor to help them work through all the issues. This showed Trang that she was serious about repairing their relationship and made him remember the devotion she had once shown him. After a good deal of time and many sessions with the counselor, Trang was able to forgive Mai. The hurt never went away completely. And neither ever forgot what had happened. But they restored their partnership and moved ahead together.

RELATIONSHIP QUIZ

To think about how forgiveness affects your relationship, answer these questions.

1. How have you hurt your partner or violated his or her trust in some way recently? How often does that happen?
2. Think about some of the recent occasions. Categorize them as big or small hurts. Big hurts might include lying about money or using something against your partner during a fight that he or she told you during an intimate exchange.

Small hurts might include angry outbursts after an event or forgetting something your partner needed.

3. Think about your examples of small hurts:
   a. What have you done to work toward forgiveness? Have you taken responsibility for your actions, tried to change, or apologized?
   b. Has your partner forgiven you for the hurt?
4. Answer the same questions about the bigger hurts you've caused your partner.
5. Now think about the big and small hurts your partner may have caused you.
   a. Are you carrying any grudges over things your partner did, perhaps years ago? If you are, why do you think you haven't been able to forgive him or her? For example, do you think the hurt was too great to forgive?
   b. Do you feel you're as open as you can be to forgiving your partner, or do you still feel justified in holding on to your anger or resentment? How do you think this affects your relationship?

THE STEPS TO FORGIVENESS

For some infractions, it's fairly easy to forgive. Your partner takes responsibility and the offense wasn't huge. You remember that your partnership is the most important thing. And you let your love and commitment guide you to letting go of the hurt or resentment.

But sometimes forgiveness just doesn't seem possible. Even if you know you should forgive, you're just not able. You need extra help to get you on the road to reconciliation.

That's where these steps can really help. They'll show you not only what you can do on your own but also what you need to do together. Working through the steps together will keep the process structured and safe, and make the repair and restoration of your partnership much more likely.

Step 1: Schedule a Couple Meeting to Discuss the Problem Issue

For a major issue, it's important to set aside time to talk about it when there's no possibility of distraction. By dealing with the issue rather than letting it slide, you will make it clear that it's having a significant effect on your relationship. A couple meeting will give you the opportunity to handle the issue thoroughly and well. Set the meeting for as soon as possible and come to it prepared to have an open, honest, respectful conversation.

Step 2: Set an Agenda for Working on the Issue

Begin by identifying the problem or the event that caused the pain. For example, the issues for Mai and Trang would be fidelity, sharing concerns, spending more time together, and how to move on after separating.

Once you've named the problem, determine that you're both ready to work on it. If you're not, wait until you are.

At the appropriate time, prepare an agenda for handling the issue. For example, you might agree to meet every Wednesday night to explore the issue and work toward forgiveness. If there are several issues to discuss, plan to work on only one at a time.

Step 3: Explore the Pain and Problems Associated with the Issue

At this point you need to have an open, caring talk about what happened and how it affected both of you. It's very important that both of you present your viewpoint and hear the other's viewpoint, and that each of you validates the other's feelings. Discuss the pain that was caused and the concerns you both have. For example, Trang might tell Mai about how painful it was to learn she had cheated on him. Mai would hear how she hurt him, and validate his feelings. She could also tell Trang that she felt terrible about what she had done.

Talking about such difficult issues requires safety and respect. If you need help to establish this kind of environment, think about using the Speaker-Listener Technique. X-Y-Z statements can also be especially helpful for expressing your feelings in a constructive way.

Throughout your discussions, be sure to listen carefully to what your partner says. Even if you're the one who's been hurt, you may hear something that can lead to a change for the better in your relationship.

Step 4: The Offending Partner Asks for Forgiveness

Once the pain and concerns have been clearly heard and understood by both partners, the offender should ask for forgiveness. Saying "I'm sorry, I was wrong. Please forgive me" can do a great deal to start the healing process.

Even if you think you haven't done anything wrong, you may still want to ask your partner to forgive you. If you've fully discussed the issue, you'll realize why your partner felt hurt. And though you may not agree that you did anything wrong to cause it, you can still ask for forgiveness for the pain your partner felt. This can be very hard to do, but it's critical for restoring your relationship.

Apologizing and asking for forgiveness are a large part of taking responsibility. You don't have to beat yourself up, but you do need to take this powerful step to show your continuing love and respect.

Step 5: The Person Who Has Been Hurt
Agrees to Forgive

Once the offending party has apologized and asked for forgiveness, the person who has been hurt should indicate the intention to forgive. Making this intention clear gives weight to the decision and makes you both accountable for repairing the relationship.

When you forgive, you're saying that you plan to put the damaging event behind you. You're saying you won't bring it up again in the middle of future arguments and that you won't keep holding it against your partner.

It doesn't mean, however, that you won't feel any more pain or other effects from the event. For example, Trang felt great pain for some time after he forgave Mai for cheating on him. But it does mean you will work toward restoring the relationship and healing the wounds.

Step 6: The Offender Commits to Changing Damaging Patterns or Attitudes

This step isn't needed in every circumstance. But if there's a specific behavior problem that keeps recurring and causing trouble, the offender needs to commit to breaking the pattern and correcting it.

For example, Dave forgot about one important meeting. It wasn't a habit for him, and it never happened again. But if he had missed several wedding meetings, it would be appropriate for Melanie to ask him to change the hurtful pattern. She would need him to do that to show that he was truly committed to her and wanted the wedding to take place. Then he would have to follow through by going to every appointment. In addition to changing the damaging pattern, Dave could also make amends by doing something special for Melanie, such as bringing her a flower each time they went to a wedding meeting or suggesting a spectacular honeymoon trip they hadn't thought of before.

Step 7: Move Forward

The first six steps will help enormously to get your relationship back on track. By following them, you'll explore the problems, validate the pain, ask for and, we hope, receive forgiveness, and commit to restoring your relationship.

Now it's time to put the event behind you. The healing process may take a long time. In fact, it may take many months or even years, as it did for Trang and Mai. But as you heal, it's important to leave the event behind you and move forward together. Rather than let it hold you back, choose instead to get beyond it as a team. We think you'll be very glad you did.

Help Yourself Forgive

Research on forgiveness suggests two powerful ways that make it more likely you'll fully forgive your partner.

1. Develop some empathy. Put yourself in your partner's shoes, and really feel all the stresses and strains he or she might have been experiencing. Try to see how the problem came about from your partner's point of view, even if what was done is clearly wrong. For example, doing this could help Trang understand how his working more increased Mai's loneliness.

2. Think a bit about how you've made mistakes in your life and how you've hurt others from time to time, including your partner. If you have the humility to recognize that you've hurt others, you're more likely to be able to forgive others who have hurt you.

MAKING AMENDS

An additional way to work toward forgiveness is to do things that demonstrate your wish to restore your relationship. These "peace offerings" shouldn't be thought of as debt paying or as a plea for forgiveness, but as positive acts that show your commitment and love.

For example, after some time had gone by, Mai might have invited Trang to a romantic weekend away. A goodwill gesture you might make could be taking over some of your spouse's chores, pampering him or her in some way (from back rubs to time at a spa), or bringing home a small gift. A caring, thoughtful act can help move you along the road to restoration.

REGAINING TRUST

If you're motivated and committed to your marriage, it's likely you'll be able to forgive your partner for most of the hurt he or she causes.

But what if something major happens that really damages your faith in your partner? You may eventually be able to forgive. But how can you ever restore your trust?

When Mai had an affair, Trang's trust in her was broken. Eventually he did forgive her. But it took nearly two years before he felt he could rely on her and believe her again.

Regaining trust after an extremely damaging event can be hard. Here are two points to consider as you go about that work.

1. *It's going to take time.* Deep trust develops from knowing that your partner is there for you over a very long period. When that trust is broken, it may take another long time to rebuild. Even if you forgive, the pain you felt may make you wary of trusting—and being hurt—again.

2. *Both partners need to take responsibility for their actions.* Mai needs to take responsibility for her behavior and for restoring the relationship, and so does Trang. Mai needs to do everything she can to show her commitment to her husband and to change her old behavior. Trang needs to show Mai that he's not going to hold the affair against her forever. Both partners must work to close the distance between them. And both need to genuinely want to move ahead together.

To rebuild trust, both partners need to work hard to show their dedication. They also need to commit to living together in new ways. One of the best things the offending partner can do is to make sure that no other breach of trust takes place. For example, if Mai ever has another relationship with a man, it's probable that Trang will never trust her again.

MAINTAINING A FORGIVING ATTITUDE

As you go through life together, it's important to remember that forgiveness isn't a one-time thing. We congratulate you if you've been able to forgive your partner for a past offense, big or small. But guess what?

Most likely it won't be the only time you'll need to. We all forget things. We all say things we shouldn't. We make mistakes. Even when we don't intend to, we can cause pain.

If you're going to make it to home plate, you're going to need to make forgiveness a continuing, important part of your partnership. In fact, you may need to forgive daily, and do it graciously and willingly. Research shows that couples are more able to heal from even the biggest wounds when they make forgiveness and reconciliation the main theme of their relationship.

Research also shows that what motivates forgiveness may be as important as forgiveness itself. If it's done for personal benefit, the effects don't hold up well over the long term. What makes the positive effects of forgiveness last is the authentic love you feel for your partner and your desire to preserve the relationship.

None of us is perfect, so acceptance needs to be a big ingredient of your forgiveness. Say, for example, that you've been married for a while and you've always wished your partner shared your love of golfing. She just never got into it, though. And you've been holding a grudge about it for some time.

If you look at the situation with an attitude of forgiveness, you'll see that being a golfer just isn't part of who she is. You can keep holding it against her. But that will be damaging to your relationship. Instead, think about forgiving what you think of as a failing, and concentrate on all her great points (we think there'll be a lot). Partners should definitely try to please each other. But for those habits, traits, or characteristics that can't be changed, acceptance and forgiveness are key.

⚡ POWER-UP EXERCISES

INDIVIDUAL EXERCISE

Take out your notebook and think and write about what in the chapter had the greatest effect on you.

COUPLE EXERCISE

Schedule time to work on an issue that needs forgiveness. Talk safely and respectfully about the issue, following the seven-step process in this chapter. We suggest that you start with a less serious issue. Then, using all the guidelines and techniques you've learned so far, work up to handling the more important issues. You'll gain confidence and learn to go forward as a team.

PART IV

SAFE AT HOME

S core one for your team! You've made it around the bases. You've learned how to handle conflict, have fun together, enhance your love life, forgive each other, and take all the other steps that are key to creating a great marriage.

In this part of the program, we focus on two areas that will help keep your marriage safe at home year after year: friendship and commitment. Both generally start out strong in most marriages. But often they can slip away, leaving partners detached and with no sense of dedication. We'll show you how to stay good friends if you're pals and confidants now. And we'll show you how to become best friends again if your relationship has lost its way.

We've saved commitment for last because it's probably the most important part of our program. We believe it's the glue that holds marriages together, and it gives you the best chance of staying a happy team for years to come. In Hour 12 we'll show you how to dedicate or rededicate yourselves to your relationship. And we'll show you how to stay safe at home by being mindful of your commitment every day.

Being Friends

WHAT WOULD YOU SAY IS THE THING YOU WANT MOST FROM YOUR MAR-
RIAGE? Most people we've asked—both men and women, and of all
ages and backgrounds—answered the same thing: to have a friend who
will be there for them.

Couples get together because they want the happiness, fun, and
intimacy that come from being best friends. They want someone who
will listen to them, support them, respect them, and love them. They
want someone they can relax with and who will accept them for who
they are.

When partners marry, they often describe their partner as their
best friend. In fact, many couples start out as friends, and develop a
romantic relationship later. The connection is strong because the two
are there for each other and create a safe haven in an often difficult
world.

With time, though, the role of friend can get buried under all the
roles a partner may take on: husband or wife, parent, coworker, club

president, soccer coach, problem solver, teacher, and on and on. But it is extremely important that friendship stays strong in your marriage. Research indicates that people who have at least one really good friend do better throughout their lives in just about every way. Although it's definitely important to have friends outside your marriage, being friends with your partner will make you both happier and more satisfied with life.

In earlier hours we pointed out the importance of fun, physical intimacy, and forgiveness in a healthy and fulfilling relationship. In this hour we urge you to add friendship to the list.

A Few Thoughts on Friendship

The only way to have a friend is to be one.

—POET RALPH WALDO EMERSON

In the sweetness of friendship, let there be laughter and the sharing of pleasures. For in the dew of little things the heart finds its morning and is refreshed.

—AUTHOR AND PHILOSOPHER KAHLIL GIBRAN

And the song, from beginning to end, I found in the heart of a friend.

—POET HENRY WADSWORTH LONGFELLOW

A faithful friend is the medicine of life.

—THE BIBLE

Friendship is a sheltering tree.

—POET SAMUEL TAYLOR COLERIDGE

Hold a true friend with both your hands.

—NIGERIAN PROVERB

Friendship is a single soul dwelling in two bodies.

—PHILOSOPHER ARISTOTLE

This communicating of a man's self to his friend works two contrary effects; for it redoubleth joys and cutteth griefs in half.

—AUTHOR AND PHILOSOPHER SIR FRANCIS BACON

THE MANY ASPECTS OF FRIENDSHIP

Different people have different definitions of the word *friend*. Some think it's a person you can trust. Some think it's a person to have fun with. Others think a friend is someone who will help and support you. Still others think a friend is a soul mate who shares what's in your heart. One of our favorite definitions comes from a colleague of ours, Bill Coffin. He calls a friend "someone who's happy to see you and doesn't have any immediate plans for your improvement."

A friend is all these things and more. But whatever your definition, it's likely you want to have one. Friendship is a powerful way to feel deeply connected to another person, to care for and assist another person, and to feel loved and protected.

When couples marry, they often say they're marrying their best friend, even though they may still be getting to know each other. They anticipate that they'll be able to let down their hair, express their most important dreams and feelings, and share fears as well as fun. They also think that no matter what, their friend will understand.

Friendship is one of the top expectations that people have for marriage. They assume that when they marry they're connecting with a best friend for life. That's why when friendship fails in a marriage, the marriage often fails. Without friendship, partners feel isolated, lonely, unsafe, and disconnected.

Men and women do share as friends, but they do it in different ways. Women generally connect as friends by talking face-to-face. Men usually talk as friends while doing an activity together.

But that's not the reason that friendship can erode over the course of a marriage. The main barriers to spousal friendship are

- Lack of time
- Thinking of yourselves as only husband and wife rather than as friends as well
- Not taking part in friendship talk, but only discussing problems, concerns, and everyday issues

- Letting conflict get in the way
- Saying destructive things to each other that lead to a lack of intimacy

Let's take a closer look at each barrier. Then we'll show you ways to overcome them.

Lack of Time

OK. We know. You have a million things to do. You have to go to work, drive the carpool, shovel the snow, buy the groceries, exercise, call your mom, be a lover, fix the leak, do the laundry, and on and on and on. When there's so much to handle, and so many everyday responsibilities, doing things as friends can get pushed to the end of the priority list.

It was probably a lot easier to relax and have fun as friends when you first met. You found more time for it, because it's likely you didn't have as many responsibilities then. But as life goes on and more things get added to the mix, it can be very hard to find the time to just enjoy being together.

Thinking of Yourselves as Husband and Wife, Not Friends

Lots of couples have told us that they were friends with their spouse when they were dating. Then they got married, which means they're not friends any longer, they're husband and wife.

Many people mistakenly believe that once you're married, you can't be friends. The new roles put you in different positions. But the couples in the strongest marriages we've come across over the years say that friendship is the basis of their relationship. These partners tell us they started out as friends and never let that bond go. They continue to share just about everything in their lives and maintain a relationship built on deep acceptance, forgiveness, caring, and safety. Some of them have been married 40 or 50 years or longer.

Not Participating in Friendship Talk

Back in Hour 3 we told you about the three kinds of talking couples do: casual talking, talking about conflict, and talking as friends. We showed you then how important friendship talk is for keeping and strengthening your connection.

To be friends, you need to talk as friends. Probably you already talk to friends other than your spouse about things you enjoy and do. But it can be harder to talk to your spouse in that way when you need to discuss a crisis at work, who needs to make a dental appointment, what thank-you gift to give your neighbor, the continuing problem about credit card debt, and all the other issues and activities you're both involved in. Suddenly you may find that you talk only about problems and arrangements, and no longer share your innermost thoughts, feelings, and interests.

Talking About Your Relationship

Friendship talk can be about anything that's important or enjoyable: movies, goals, dreams, sports, music, something that strikes you funny, books, a secret desire, hobbies, you name it. However, studies show that women are generally more comfortable and interested in talking with friends about their relationship than men are.

In one study, women were asked to talk with a female friend about concerns in their marriage. Men were asked to do the same thing with a male friend. The researcher, Danielle Julien, from the University of Quebec at Montreal, explained what happened: "... the wife-friend conversations look[ed] like happy fishes swimming in fresh water. Talking about relationships seemed so natural and enjoyable to them that we often had to interrupt them because they would never stop. Several husband-friend conversations looked uneasy, and we surely never had to interrupt them: their conversations were short."

If talking as friends about certain areas makes one of you uncomfortable, switch to something you both enjoy. Save concerns or discussions about your relationship for couple meetings. But after spending pleasant time together as friends, you may both feel comfortable enough to talk about anything.

Letting Conflict Get in the Way

Earlier in the book we talked about how conflict can get in the way of having fun and having sex. If it isn't handled well and at appropriate moments, conflict can ruin your good times and lead to anger and unhappiness.

It's also possible for conflict to keep you from being friends. If you've just argued and gotten upset over something, it's pretty unlikely that the two of you are going to feel like friends just then. In fact, you might feel like enemies. Then you might have a hard time reconnecting as friends.

We believe that conflict is one of the main reasons couples talk less and less as friends over the course of their marriage. They allow their issues to tear apart their friendship.

Take Billy Ray and Jolene. They had been married for 16 years, but had never had much money for vacations. When they were first married, they had enjoyed going camping together. But with a teenage son and lots of obligations, even that kind of inexpensive outing didn't happen often.

When Jolene's parents retired, they offered to take their grandson Jack on a short fishing trip. He was excited to go. So Billy Ray and Jolene decided to take the opportunity to go camping at a nearby park.

The first night, after a great day of hiking and a cozy campfire dinner, their conversation went like this.

JOLENE: It is so wonderful to be out in the mountains again. I've really missed getting away like this.

BILLY RAY: Isn't it great? I'm probably going to be sore tomorrow. But that lake we hiked up to was fantastic. It felt so good to cool off in the water and then lie in the sun.

JOLENE: I loved it too. The whole area is gorgeous. And the campgrounds are so clean and private. This place has just about everything.

BILLY RAY: It really does. *(sitting down next to Jolene and putting his arm around her)* About the only thing missing that I can think of is a little music.

JOLENE: *(laughing and snuggling with Billy Ray)* Some romantic music *would* be nice. You know, speaking of music, we never really talked about Jack wanting to take guitar lessons. He really wants to learn.

BILLY RAY: *(tensing up a bit)* We didn't talk about it, Jo, because we can't afford it. You should know that.

JOLENE: But we might be able to borrow a guitar, and then it would just be the cost of the lessons. I could look into it. Maybe they wouldn't be too much.

BILLY RAY: *(getting annoyed)* Whatever it costs, it's too much. Let's just not talk about it.

JOLENE: *(getting upset too)* You never want to talk about anything. You always think the worst. How do you know there's not some way to work it out? I'd really like to do this for him.

BILLY RAY: *(very angry)* You want to do everything for him. I don't think he does enough for himself. He's got to learn to take on more responsibility.

JOLENE: *(very angry too)* He's very responsible. He's a great kid. But since you always think the worst, I'm sure I won't be able to change your mind. I'm going to sleep. *(She gets up and stomps into the tent.)*

Do you see what happened here? Things started out well. Billy Ray and Jolene enjoyed a day of hiking and then relaxed over dinner. But then they let their differences of opinion ruin their fun. Their conversation escalated, and issues about money, negative thinking, and responsibility were triggered. What began as a great talk between friends turned into an argument.

Arguments are bad enough. But something else damaging can result when conflict gets in the way. A great many couples have told us that they get nervous when they think about spending time together. If one conversation ended in a fight, the next one could too. And the next and the next. If you're worried that every time you're with your partner things could get ugly, you may stop wanting to be with your partner at all.

Saying Destructive Things

One of the biggest barriers to friendship between spouses springs up when words are used as weapons. For example, in the middle of a very intimate discussion, you might share some feelings about a past partner. Years later, during an argument, your partner might throw those old feelings in your face.

If that happens, are you going to feel safe enough to share your deepest feelings again? Probably not. Are you going to want to protect yourself instead of reveal yourself? Probably you are. Turning your partner's words against him or her is a sure way to keep you from being friends.

RELATIONSHIP QUIZ

Answer these questions about friendship in your marriage.

1. Do you think of your partner as a friend? Your best friend?
2. Are there things you would tell another friend that you wouldn't share with your partner? If so, why do you think you wouldn't express those thoughts or feelings?

3. Think back to the last activity you did as a couple. Did you have fun together the entire time? Or did an issue come up that turned some of your conversation into an argument?
4. Remember a recent time you spent with a friend who isn't your spouse. What kinds of things did you talk about? Did you share feelings or dreams? Laugh? Feel safe enough to say anything? Can you imagine having that same kind of conversation with your spouse?
5. Is some time each week devoted to relaxing and having fun with your partner as friends?

PROTECTING YOUR FRIENDSHIP

By now you've probably gotten the point that friendship is extremely important for a great marriage. If you and your partner are already the best of companions, we want you to keep making that powerful connection a priority. The following suggestions will help you sustain your special link.

But maybe, as you've been reading this chapter and taking the quiz, you've been wondering where your best friend has gone. Maybe you've been thinking, "A lot of those barriers have been built up in our relationship. We never seem to have the time to talk about interests the way we used to. I guess I don't think of us as friends—we seem more like appointment makers and activity directors."

It happens to a lot of couples. But you can both make changes now to put friendship back in your marriage. Here's how to do it:

- Make the time to have fun as friends.
- Keep friendship time safe from conflict.
- Talk as friends.

The following strategies will help you get started.

Make the Time for Having Fun as Friends

Research has shown us that most partners want to be better friends. Once they discover how important it is, they want to start improving their friendship immediately. Friendship is a natural tendency for most of us. So even if it's been ignored or shut down, it's possible to bring it back to life and then nurture and protect it.

We definitely hope that you already spend a lot of time together doing things you enjoy, not just things that have to be taken care of. This is a great way to nurture your friendship and build a lasting connection.

But even if you currently do many things as friends, we suggest you set aside specific times for friendship activities. When schedules get busy, it can be hard to fit in time for relaxation and fun. You may think you'll be able to do it, but life may get in the way. If you plan for it, it's more likely to actually happen.

To make friendship time a regular part of your week, note it right in your calendar. Schedule it like any other important activity. Then make sure you use the time to be together, without distractions or conflict. If you look at your calendar and think, "There's just no time," make some. If you have to, carve out an hour or two from other activities. Or say no to something you've been considering doing. Make time together a priority.

Just what should you do during friendship time? Anything you both enjoy. This could be as inexpensive and relatively easy to arrange as sitting and talking in a relaxing place about things that are important to you. Or it could be combining intimate conversation with an activity, such as taking a walk or going out dancing. You could share a great meal, take a drive, spend time on a hobby, choose a new interest to pursue together, or play cards or go camping. The idea is to be together as friends, in whatever way or place that helps it happen.

Keep Friendship Time Safe from Conflict

In Part One of this book, we talked a lot about how important it is to handle conflict well. One of the main reasons it's so important is that it protects all the great things about your marriage from the damage conflict can cause.

Having and being a friend are definitely great parts of being married. So you need to keep your friendship from harm by keeping conflict out of your friendship time. To do that, schedule regular times to talk about issues and potential conflicts. Use the techniques covered throughout the book, including the Speaker-Listener Technique and the Time Out, to help with difficult discussions. Also agree to the ground rule about not letting conflict interfere with pleasurable times.

Another way you can keep your friendship safe is to forgive each other for past hurts. If during conflict either of you ever brought up personal information the other partner shared during friendship time, ask for forgiveness and take responsibility for never doing it again. Resentment, bitterness, and disappointment can lead to arguments and disconnection if you can't forgive your partner for what caused those painful feelings. No matter the size of the hurt, we believe it's possible to forgive your partner and move on as friends.

One strategy that helps many couples keep conflict at bay is for them to agree they'll always be in friendship-talk mode until they decide to change to another way of talking. That means that whatever is going on, they're going to talk as friends. They simply won't discuss issues. When concerns need to be dealt with, they set aside time for doing so and use conflict talk during their meeting.

Other couples choose to designate certain times as friendship times. For example, when they're heading out to dinner together or for a walk, one of them will say, "Let's make this friendship time, OK?" That makes the time off-limits from concerns or disagreements.

By keeping issues in their place, you'll keep your friendship strong.

Talk as Friends

This may seem like a no-brainer. But when partners marry, they often start thinking like spouses or parents and forget to think and act like friends. The key here is to remember that you can be a spouse and a parent *and* a friend.

Friends . . .

- Listen without blame or anger
- Show respect for each other's opinions, even if they disagree
- Are interested in each other and what happens to each other
- Don't compete in ways that lead to rejection or tension
- Share common passions and beliefs
- Make each other feel safe
- Don't try to change each other

Do you talk and listen to your partner as a friend? What exactly does that mean? Here are some pointers for being together as friends:

• *Talk without fighting.* Think about how you spend time with other women and men friends. Do you argue a lot? You might have a small disagreement about something, but you don't let it build, and you don't let it get in the way of your good time. You're careful to protect your relationship and not to hurt each other's feelings.

Do the same thing with your husband or wife. When you're spending time together as friends, talk as friends, not as enemies.

• *Don't focus on solving problems.* When you spend time with your other friends, you probably don't try to solve a lot of problems. You might exchange ideas on how to fit more exercise into your schedule or discuss trouble you've been having at work, but you don't tackle big issues when you're together to have fun.

The same thing should go when you're spending friendship time with your spouse. Keep it for talking about topics that can bring you closer. Use your couple meetings for discussing issues and solving any problems.

• *Listen like a friend.* Do you feel as though you can say just about anything to your friends? Probably you do, because you feel safe and accepted when you're with them.

You and your spouse can feel the same way in each other's company. You can say what you think and have your partner listen without judgment. Friends care about what each other says and feels, and listen without being defensive.

When friends listen to friends, they focus on who they are, what they care about, what their dreams are, the things they enjoy, what worries them, and all the other things that make them the people they are. Friends listen even when the topic isn't something that interests them, because it interests their friend. It's a sacrifice you make to be a good friend.

Friends also accept each other for who they are. They don't try to change each other, they just try to relax and have a good time. They also don't offer advice unless it's asked for. Friends don't want someone to tell them what to do as much as they want to be heard and appreciated.

One of the best gifts you can give to your partner is to be his or her friend.

POWER-UP EXERCISES

INDIVIDUAL EXERCISE

Take out your notebook and think and write about what in this hour had the greatest effect on you.

Then take some time to think about how to strengthen and protect the friendship in your relationship. Think about your schedule—where could you make time for friendship? What arrangements would you need to make, such as finding a baby-sitter?

COUPLE EXERCISE

Schedule some time to talk safely and respectfully about friendship in your marriage. Use the Speaker-Listener Technique if you need it. Focus on why you want to protect your friendship and on accepting the ground rule about protecting the great things in your life from conflict. Then make plans for how you'll spend some friendship time and block it out on your planners.

The idea behind friendship time is to have quiet, uninterrupted periods just to be together and talk as friends. You probably have lots of ideas for what to talk about during these special moments. But when you get together to talk, the following suggestions can get things under way. Just remember to avoid all conflict and problem solving.

- *Talk about an event or something important from your childhood.* It might be something you've been thinking about or something you'd just like to share. You can reveal something about your family, your schooling, friends—whatever jumps to mind.

- *Discuss a current goal or something you've always dreamed of doing or being.* Or talk about something personal you may not have felt safe enough to talk about before.

- *Talk about something you're involved in or interested in now.* It might be a project at work, a book you're reading, new music you just heard, a newspaper article, your hobby, a movie, or a club you're thinking of joining.

- *Express your views on current events.* You could discuss how your favorite team is doing, the local or national political scene, the state of education, the party you're going to this weekend, a new store that's coming to your neighborhood, or anything that's going on around town or somewhere in the world.

- *Interview each other.* Ask your partner about his or her life. You can ask about earliest memories, funny incidents, favorite pets, family traditions or vacations, the first time driving a car, what he or she wanted to be as a grownup, early playmates, teenage fears, things that annoy him or her now, all-time favorite movies—anything that shows your partner's personal side.

Good interviewers draw out their interviewee by asking open-ended questions, ones that can't be answered with a yes or a no. They also ask questions that help them understand the person, and listen to the answers with a generous and sensitive ear. By interviewing your partner, you may learn something "beautiful and new," as the song "Getting to Know You" proclaims, as well as have a great time together.

Making the Commitment

HERE YOU ARE AT THE LAST HOUR OF THE PREP PROGRAM! Doesn't the time fly when you're doing something positive, exciting, and fun?! Now you have just one more subject to cover, one that will help you stick instead of feel stuck.

That subject is commitment. It's a word that's used a lot these days, especially in relationship to business and activities. "He's so committed to his job." "She made the commitment, so she'll show up." "We've committed to buying 20 tickets for the fundraiser."

Commitment is crucial to marriage as well. In fact, it may be the most important ingredient in the recipe for marital success. Pledging yourselves to each other and promising to love and support each other until you die can hold you together like no other glue. There is great power in a commitment made between two loving people.

On their wedding day, all couples commit to each other. And, most likely, they mean what they say. As they kiss and head back down the aisle, they intend to stay together happily for as long as they live.

Over time, though, some couples forget or ignore the commitment they made. For any number of reasons, they become unhappy or disenchanted. Then, instead of remembering their commitment and rededicating themselves to their marriage and their partner, they may think about separation or divorce. Once partners stop acting on their commitment, their marriage is more likely to go downhill in ways they never dreamed of when they married.

Commitment shouldn't be something that's only honored for the length of your honeymoon. Like friendship, which we explored in Hour 11, commitment needs to be nurtured and demonstrated every day. If you want a long and happy marriage, which we're sure you do, you need to be good friends with your partner and to stay deeply committed to your relationship.

If you're already following through on your commitment and building a strong, nurturing relationship, the information in this hour will help you continue to honor it and make your marriage thrive. If your commitment has weakened, the strategies we describe can help you come together again, rather than come undone.

TWO KINDS OF COMMITMENT

When you think about being committed to your partner, what comes to mind? You might think about pledging yourself or making a promise to him or her. But you might not know that there are two kinds of commitment that work to keep partners in a relationship. One we call *personal dedication* and the other *constraint commitment*.

1. *Personal dedication.* Personal dedication refers to a promise—and the actions to fulfill that promise—to maintain and improve a relationship for the mutual benefit of both partners. This involves going beyond simply continuing in the relationship but actively doing what it takes to increase its quality: investing in it, sacrificing for it, linking it to personal goals, and seeking to improve not only your own welfare but your partner's as well.

2. *Constraint commitment.* This type of commitment refers to one enforced by circumstances rather than by the partners themselves. Whether or not partners are dedicated to their relationship, outside or internal forces work to keep them in it, and can make relationships more stable. Particular constraints will vary depending on the kind of people partners are, what they value, and the circumstances they're in. Common factors that constrain couples are

- Social pressure from friends and family
- Financial considerations
- Not wanting to split up property or valuables
- Concern for their children or the fear of loss of contact with them
- The difficulties involved in actually ending the relationship
- Moral conflicts, such as the belief that divorce is wrong or that a person should always finish what he or she started
- Alternatives thought of as less attractive, such as living alone or having less money
- Concern for the partner's welfare

The higher the number of constraints, the more likely it is that a partner will choose to stay in a marriage, even if dedication decreases.

Examples of Commitment

To understand the two types of commitment and their effects, let's take a look at two very different couples. The first couple thrives on their personal dedication to staying married and supporting and loving each other. The other started out happily, but let the stresses of life overpower their commitment. Their marriage is now held together by constraints rather than devotion.

> Vincent and Julie have been married for 10 years. They have three young children, ages eight, six, and four. Julie stays at

home with the kids. Vincent is a foreman for a commercial construction company.

Before they met, Vincent had dated a number of other women. But when he started seeing Julie, he knew she was the one. He told her his dating days were over, and he committed to spending the rest of his life with her.

Over the two years he and Julie dated, Vincent proved his devotion. Julie was equally committed to being with Vincent. When they took their marriage vows, both were very confident that their marriage was forever. And they've both worked hard to make that goal a reality.

Their life together hasn't been easy. Vincent was badly hurt in a construction fall. Their middle child has learning disabilities. Julie is often exhausted, and she wonders if she'll ever be able to get back to the merchandising career she loved. And as with so many couples, money is often very tight.

But through it all, Julie and Vincent have been there for each other. Both took their commitment to be loving partners seriously. To maintain their strong connection, they make time to be together on their own, to talk to each other about feelings and concerns, to enjoy each other's company as friends, to help each other out, and to keep romance and passion alive.

Sometimes Vincent meets other women he thinks are attractive. Julie sometimes daydreams about a prince who will carry her away from the endless piles of laundry, the spilled juice, and the arguments over toys. But even when things are at their worst, neither of them thinks about divorce. They choose to focus on their marriage and not consider other options. They remember that they came together because they love and respect each other, and they're committed to staying the course.

Vincent and Julie have a strong sense of dedication to each other, which helps them through difficult times. Like all couples, they also have some constraints: concern for their children and fear of being alone, to name two. But what really makes their marriage work is their desire to stay together and the energy they put into it.

Priscilla and Erik have been married nearly 22 years. They have twin teenage boys who will be leaving for college soon. Priscilla works full-time as a copywriter, and Erik is an account executive.

Erik and Priscilla fell in love quickly. Living in a large city, they had spent weekends having romantic dinners and going to museums, sporting events, and all kinds of shows and concerts. Priscilla thought Erik was adventurous and charming. Erik thought Priscilla was creative, loving, and great fun to be with. Within a year they had married.

The two were committed, and they set out to have a great life together. But within a few years, things had changed. Erik was asked to set up and head a new office for his company in a different city. It was a great promotion for him, so reluctantly Priscilla agreed to move.

Erik jumped right into his new job and loved it. But Priscilla wasn't able to find a new job she enjoyed. Then she learned she was pregnant with twins, so she decided to put off looking for work.

The years went by. A lot of it was great. The family spent as much time as they could together, and had the money to travel and live comfortably. But Erik continued to work a lot of nights and weekends to develop his business. Priscilla never went back to work and was very involved with her children's activities and her church.

As the boys' senior year of high school started, Priscilla began to worry. For the last few years she had felt more and more distant from Erik. They hardly ever went out as a couple. And they had started to disagree about a lot of things.

Now, whenever they were alone, she worried that an argument would start. She always felt uncomfortable. Soon it would be just the two of them, and the thought of it was depressing. Several of her friends had decided to divorce when they became empty-nesters. She wondered if that was the right thing for her too.

Without saying so, Erik felt pretty much the same way. Both partners felt unappreciated, worried, discouraged, and unhappy.

But when each separately thought of divorce, a number of things stopped them from bringing it up. Both loved their children enormously and didn't want to do anything that would hurt them. Priscilla also worried that because she had been out of the job market so long it would be next to impossible to find a good position. She thought she would get some alimony, but it probably wouldn't be enough to enable her to live the way she'd been living. And she knew her parents wouldn't approve. She and her family were very religious, and it had been ingrained in her that divorce was wrong. In addition, both Priscilla and Erik had put a lot of effort into making their home special, and they realized they wouldn't be able to keep it if they ended their marriage.

The more they thought about it, the more both thought that no matter how unhappy they were, divorcing would

> result in their losing out on a number of things that were very important to one or both of them. Their constraints kept them married. But because they didn't discuss and work on their issues, and didn't make the decision to rededicate themselves to each other and their marriage, they both remained miserable.

Erik and Priscilla's marriage is now held together only by constraint commitment. Both have lost the sense of "us" they used to have, and they've done nothing to rededicate themselves to their relationship. They will probably stay married, but only because they feel pressured to do so by outside circumstances. Neither feels personally committed to their marriage.

This doesn't have to be the end of their story, however. By following the suggestions we give in this hour, especially in the section "Rediscovering Dedication," Erik and Priscilla can rebuild their marriage into a much more satisfying one based on deep personal dedication. You can too.

HOW COMMITMENT GROWS

The more partners enjoy being together, the more they commit to their relationship. For example, when you first started going out together, you may have liked each other but might not have been ready to say, "This is it. You're the one, and I'm not going to date anyone else."

Then, after a while, your love began to grow. You relaxed and had fun. You really hit it off. You may have been a bit worried about whether you would stay together. But the more you sensed that your partner loved you too, the more able you were to invest in the relationship. As you both showed your love, your dedication to the relationship got stronger. Any insecurity you may have felt about the future of your relationship was eased by your mutual commitment.

In most relationships, almost all forms of commitment can be looked at as symbols of security. And when you share a deep sense of security, you will feel safer and safer at home.

HOW COMMITMENT ERODES

Just as mutual enjoyment makes commitment grow, lack of enjoyment makes commitment erode. As we've said, one of the biggest causes of dissatisfaction is conflict. When conflict isn't handled well, marital satisfaction declines, and with it personal dedication. When couples feel little commitment, they stop helping each other and doing things to make each other happy. Soon the relationship can be in trouble, with only constraint commitment holding it together.

One secret to a satisfying marriage is keeping commitment strong—not only constraint commitment but personal dedication. Constraint commitment can add a positive dimension to your marriage, stabilizing it if it starts to wobble. But it is your personal dedication that will allow you to not just exist in your relationship but thoroughly enjoy it.

Showing Your Dedication _____

In many marriages, commitment does erode. In many others, commitment stays high, only the partners don't know it. We've seen an awful lot of marriages that have lost their spark because the partners didn't express or notice their dedication.

One way this happens is that partners stop doing the things they used to do to show how much they care, such as calling in the middle of the day to say "I can't wait for tonight," surprising their partner with tickets to a play or a playoff game, doing a chore they know their partner doesn't have the energy to do, or making their anniversary a major celebration.

Commitment also erodes when both partners continue to show dedication but neither one notices. We can all become so busy or distracted that we take for granted the everyday things which show that our partner cares.

If you think your mate isn't dedicated, first ask yourself if you're negatively interpreting the situation. If you are, you can end up invalidating all your partner's efforts to protect your relationship. To counter negative interpretations, push yourself to look for signs that show your partner really cares. Also remember to make your own dedication visible. Think about and act on things you used to do but don't do much now that show you're committed to your partnership.

RELATIONSHIP QUIZ

How important are constraint commitments in your partnership? Are you both dedicated? Although it's worthwhile to think about the level of constraint commitment in your relationship, it's far more important to consider your level of personal dedication to your partner. That's because dedication is what you have the most control over. Dedication is all about the choices you make and working to make your relationship all that it can be.

Before we look more deeply at dedication, here's a quiz you can take to get a rough sense of how your dedication measures up. For each item, jot down the number that indicates how true the statement is to you. Use this scale: 1 = Strongly disagree; 4 = Neither agree nor disagree; 7 = Strongly agree.

_____ My relationship with my partner is more important to me than almost anything else in my life.

_____ I want this relationship to stay strong no matter what rough times we may encounter.

_____ It makes me feel good to sacrifice for my partner.

_____ I like to think of myself and my partner more in terms of "us" and "we" than "me" and "him [her]."

_____ I am not seriously attracted to anyone other than my partner.

_____ My relationship with my partner is clearly part of my future life plans.

_____ When push comes to shove, my relationship with my partner comes first.

_____ I tend to think about how things affect us as a couple more than how things affect me as an individual.

_____ I don't often find myself thinking about what it would be like to be in a relationship with someone else.

_____ I want to grow old with my partner.

Now total your responses. If you have a score higher than 58, you are probably pretty dedicated to your marriage. A score of less than 45 suggests pretty low dedication, and you might find the section on rededicating yourself to your relationship especially helpful. Don't jump there now, though. Just read on.

FOUR KEYS TO STAYING PERSONALLY COMMITTED

Our research has shown that four key factors are at the core of personal dedication in the strongest relationships:

1. Making the right choices
2. Strengthening and preserving your identity as a couple
3. Making sacrifices
4. Wanting and expecting your relationship to last

By choosing to do these things, you and your partner can stay safe at home. Let's take a look at why each is important.

Making the Right Choices

People are faced with choices in every part of their lives. Marriage is no exception. Being committed to your marriage means that you're going to need to make two key choices that can make or break your relationship: the choice to make your relationship a priority every day and the choice not to pursue a different partner.

Making Your Marriage a Priority

When couples in great marriages make decisions among competing possibilities, they choose to do the things that will protect their relationship. For example, say that on a Saturday afternoon you need to run errands, take the cat to the vet, and catch up on housework, and you'd also like to talk with a few friends. Those things need to be done, to be sure. But if you let all such things crowd out time to nurture your marriage, distance will grow between you and your spouse.

If you've been a couple for years, think back to how you used to move mountains to spend time together. Do you do it now? One of the most important ways to show your dedication is to make the time to be together as friends.

To keep your priorities straight, you may have to say no to some of the things you'd like to do. But saying yes to your spouse and making sure your relationship doesn't just occupy space around the edges of your life can help you achieve your goal of having a happy, lifelong marriage.

Dedicated people make every effort to live in ways that reflect their commitment. They think like a committed person and behave like one as well. They also don't take their partner's commitment for granted. They don't think, "Well, she'll stay with me no matter what, so I don't need to please her all the time," or "He's committed to me for life, so I can focus more on our marriage later."

Deciding the Grass Isn't Greener on the Other Side of the Fence

When you decided to be a couple, you chose to give up pursuing romantic relationships with other people. But that doesn't mean that all the other attractive people out there fell off the planet.

Have you ever thought about other partners? How seriously and how often? People who are most dedicated to their partners don't spend time thinking about what it would be like to be with someone else. Thinking about other partners is a sign of serious marital unhappiness. And it's dangerous as well.

Such thinking also usually fuels resentment in you. That's because most people think about another partner as a perfect, always positive, romantically thrilling person—not as someone they'd have to manage money, discipline children, and clean the house with. It's not a fair comparison. When you're tempted to think about being with someone else, it's likely you're not thinking all that realistically.

Instead of seriously exploring the possibility that the grass is greener somewhere else, or focusing on your partner's flaws, boost your dedication by working to make the grass grow greener on your side of the fence.

Strengthening and Preserving Your Identity as a Couple

Numerous times throughout this book, we've stressed the importance of thinking of yourselves as a couple. Although you're both individuals who need to value and preserve your own identities and do your own part to make your marriage work, you also need to think of yourselves as a team. Our research clearly shows that couples who have a strong sense of "us" have an edge when it comes to marital success.

Sometimes it's hard to maintain that feeling of being a team. You can drift apart for any number of reasons, including changes in your family (such as when children leave for college) or time-consuming, separate careers. Suddenly you may realize that each of you is really operating on your own and that you no longer think of yourselves as "us."

We hope this hasn't happened and that you're working hard to protect the home team. To maintain that important feeling of "us," or to regain a stronger sense of it, we recommend that you follow these proven strategies, which we've discussed throughout the book:

- Spend time doing activities that you both enjoy or that have deep meaning for you.
- Do the exercises in this book together.
- Talk together about what each of you can do to increase your sense of "us."
- Talk regularly about short-term and long-term goals.
- Make key decisions together.
- Develop a shared vision for your future.

Showing Your Commitment Every Day

That exciting moment when you say "I do" shouldn't be the only time you express your dedication. To stay united into the future, it's a great idea to express it every day.

To do that, think about little ways as well as big ones to show you're in this for the long haul. One way could be to come home in time for dinner with your spouse every night instead of staying late at the office. Or you could help your partner with a problem without being asked. Or say, "I love you" just because, or tell your partner how much it meant when he or she listened when you needed to think something out. By showing your partner every day that your marriage is a priority, the two of you will increase your sense of yourselves as a couple.

Making Sacrifices

There's much in our culture that encourages us to look out for number one. But there's not much encouragement to sacrifice for the good of others. Research shows, though, that selfishness damages marriage and that sacrificing for your partner can build a stronger relationship over time.

This doesn't mean you should be a doormat or give up everything that's important to you. It also doesn't mean that you should play the martyr and do things for your partner only so that he or she will owe you. It does mean that you should look for the joy that can come from choosing to do something that will make your partner happy or support him or her in some way. For example, if your spouse decides to start taking night classes to earn a degree, you can do things at home to make sure he or she has the time needed to study. In the strongest and happiest marriages, partners get deep satisfaction from doing things for each other.

Some research suggests that a sense of couple identity and a long-term view of marriage are strongly related to men's willingness to sacrifice for their female partners. We believe that historically women have given more to their marriages than men and that men without a strong sense of commitment can resent giving to women, and sometimes just won't. Male dedication levels are therefore very important to the happiness and longevity of their relationships. And men, as well as women, need to show their dedication by clearly and freely sacrificing for their mate.

If a woman doesn't see evidence that her husband is giving over a long period of time, it's possible she'll pull back. She may come to believe that her husband isn't invested in the relationship, which can make her feel demoralized about trying to connect with her partner. Hopelessness can set in, and with it the thought of divorce.

Wanting and Expecting Your Relationship to Last

We all know that no marriage is perfect and that there will be ups and downs along the way. To hang in there through the down times, both partners must believe and act as though the marriage will continue no matter what. How does that belief help? It makes you feel safe. And when you feel safe you can deal with just about anything life sends your way.

Expecting your relationship to last can also keep you from overreacting to small or annoying problems. If you truly believe that nothing can break you up, you're likely to view many problems as less than monumental, and forgive your partner for minor hurts or failings. For example, if your spouse says something unkind, most likely you'll want to discuss that it hurt you. But if you're both committed to your marriage, you probably won't see a moment of insensitivity as a major cause for alarm. You won't sweat the small stuff if you keep the long view in mind.

Believing in your future can also lead you to take risks, reveal more about yourself, and trust in your partner—all things that will increase your marital happiness. It will also encourage you to invest more in your relationship, something you probably wouldn't do if you were uncertain of where it was heading. People in general don't invest in something that's uncertain—it just doesn't make sense. But if you and your partner clearly see your future together, you're more likely to work toward making it happen by sharing dreams and goals, accepting each other's weaknesses, and cutting each other some slack when you're not at your best.

If your marriage is abusive or destructive in some way, we're not saying you should stay in it or expect it to last. But for the great number of couples who are happy with their partner and genuinely want their marriage to work, a long-term perspective is essential. It promotes the kind of safety that comes from knowing you have a future together.

There are two important ways you can support your expectation of a long and happy marriage:

• *Don't threaten it by bringing up divorce, abandonment, or having an affair.* For example, in the middle of an argument, don't say things like, "If you don't like the way I'm handling this, maybe it's time to split up." In the middle of a disagreement, don't say, "If you don't do this for me, I'm walking out." If you're having a problem about sex, don't say you're going to look for someone new. Instead of affirming the future, all such threatening words put the future at risk and erode trust and confidence. Work hard to keep these words from slipping out.

• *Do talk regularly about your dreams and goals for the future.* This might include where you'd like to be in 20 years, what you'd like to do during retirement, how you feel about becoming parents or grandparents. It doesn't mean you need to plan every step of your life or figure out every detail. But sharing your ideas or simply dreaming together reinforces the point that there is a future and that you can make it a great one by nurturing your vision together. The happiest couples in long-term marriages report that they spend a lot of time discussing what's ahead. It's a powerful way to preserve your love.

REDISCOVERING DEDICATION

If you're reading this book, it's very likely you want your marriage to last. But after reading this chapter, you may have discovered that your dedication has lessened and that constraints are mostly what are keeping you from leaving.

If that's the case, we urge you to read this section carefully. Then, if your partner is willing, we urge you to act on it. With work it's possible to renew your dedication and build your marriage into a happy one based on mutual commitment and love. But to do that, you have to really want to.

If you and your partner both want to rededicate yourselves to your marriage and are working through this book together, the following steps can help you put your marriage back on track. If you want to turn your marriage around but are working through this book on your own, you can use the following steps as a guideline, but your work will be harder. The steps are designed for two people pulling together, but we do believe that one person can do amazing things to bring life back to a marriage.

Whether you're working on your own or with your partner, you'll have to work hard, and you'll probably have to work against some of the tendencies and behaviors that have characterized your relationship so far. You'll also need to make changes to please your partner, and acknowledge, appreciate, and respect the changes he or she makes for you. And you'll need to continue making these efforts for some time.

To rededicate yourself to your marriage:

1. *Talk about the state of your marriage.* To make things better in the future, you have to face where you are right now. As you talk, try not to get defensive or to argue. Instead, work hard on really hearing and acknowledging each other's point of view. Empathize with your partner's pain. By doing so, you'll be building a bond and sharing feelings of loss or sadness. This in turn can help you rediscover intimacy, which couples in the strongest marriages share. If you need help in talking safely and respectfully about these difficult issues, you might want to use the Speaker-Listener Technique.

2. *Reminisce about all the good things you used to share.* What attracted you to each other? What did you do for fun? How did you feel on your first date? Why did you want to be a couple? Remembering and talking about such things will remind you of how you once felt about each other. Rediscovering the old spark may help reignite the embers and fuel your efforts to head in a new direction.

3. *Agree to work together to make things better.* If constraints are keeping you together unhappily, why not decide to find a way to stay together happily? Promise each other that you'll make a determined effort to rebuild what you believe you've lost. You *can* try to repair your marriage on your own, but making the commitment to do it together is far better.

4. *Do the things you used to do to show your love and protect your relationship.* If you've read the earlier hours of this program, you know how important it is to do positive things for your partnership: have fun together, talk as friends, keep passion alive, be more forgiving, have a positive outlook, meet expectations, handle conflict well. Most likely you did all these things earlier in your relationship, and they brought you together. Now it's time to do them again.

5. *Keep working on it.* Change won't happen overnight. It's going to take time, and there are going to be ups and downs. But if you both keep putting time, energy, and love into your relationship, it will all be worth it in the end. Continue to make good choices, including not looking for a new partner; develop and protect your identity as a couple; graciously sacrifice for each other; and want and expect your relationship to last.

⚡ POWER-UP EXERCISES

INDIVIDUAL EXERCISE

Take out your notebook and think and write about what in this hour had the greatest effect on you.

Then do the following exercise, which can also be used as the basis for a discussion with your partner.

Divide a piece of paper into three columns. In the first column, list the five top priorities in your life. The first thing you list should be your most important priority, and the last the least important. Priorities can include your partner, your career, children, religion, your home, goals, possessions, pets, friends, relatives—whatever is significant to you.

In the second column, list what you think your partner thinks are your five top priorities. For example, if you think your partner would say your first priority is your child, list that as number one.

In the third column, list what you think are your partner's five top priorities, again listing the most important one first.

Now take some time to look at your three columns and think about what they mean for your relationship.

COUPLE EXERCISE

When both of you have made your three lists in the individual exercise above, take the time to compare them. Consider how the answers affect you as a couple. Talk safely and respectfully, not defensively, and use the Speaker-Listener Technique if you need to. If you discover that your relationship is not a high priority for one or both of you, talk together about specific ways to move it up the scale. Review the ground rules for relationships (Hour 5) and consider using them to help get your partnership back on track. Make time to talk about how the strategies and ideas in this book can help your relationship.

Epilogue: Keeping the Program in Play

You've now officially completed the PREP 12-hour program. Congratulations! Well done! You've taken an important step toward creating a satisfying relationship that will last a lifetime.

But although the book ends here, your efforts to develop and preserve your relationship should not. To keep your marriage strong as you move forward together, you'll need to continue to practice all the skills you learned as well as reinforce all the concepts. We encourage you to reread the material often in order to master it, practice the strategies and techniques so that they become part of your life and easier to engage, and reinforce each other as you continue to exhibit positive behavior or work toward positive change.

We also urge you to be confident that your marriage will succeed. We've discovered that confidence is very important in marriage because it promotes persistence based on hope. Work on gaining confidence by putting what you've learned in this program into play. Knowledge, understanding, commitment, and confidence will help you stay the course and will bring you the deeply satisfying marriage you've dreamed of.

GETTING MORE HELP WHEN THERE ARE SERIOUS PROBLEMS

This book is based on the Prevention and Relationship Enhancement Program (PREP). PREP is an educational program that teaches you skills and principles that can help you build strong and healthy marriages and couple and family relationships. However, as an educational program, PREP is not designed to address serious relationship and individual problems.

Because you are taking this time to think more about your life and relationships, it may also be a good time to think about other services that you or others you care about may need. Even if your main goal right now is to improve your marriage or relationship, difficulties in other areas could make it that much harder to make your relationship work. Likewise, if you are having really severe problems in your relationship, it can make dealing with any of these other problems that much harder.

Here are some areas where seeking additional help could be really important for you and your family.

Financial Problems
- Serious money problems make everything else harder.
- Unemployment or job loss can be one of the key sources of conflict and stress for couples.
- Although this workshop can help you as a couple to work more as a team, you may need more help to learn to manage your finances or find a job.

Serious Marital or Other Family Problems or Stresses
- If you have serious marital or adult relationship problems for which more help is needed than can be provided in this book,

you can seek counseling from someone who specializes in helping couples.

- Coping with a serious, life-threatening or chronic illness or disability in a child or adult can place a lot of stress on caregivers and their family relationships. Community resources often exist to help families with these kinds of issues.

Substance Abuse, Addictions, and Other Compulsive Behaviors

- No matter what else you have to deal with in life, it will be harder if you, your partner, or another close family member has a substance abuse problem.
- Drug or alcohol abuse and addiction robs a person of the ability to handle life well, have close relationships, and be a good parent.
- Alcohol abuse can also make it harder to control anger and violence.
- Other problems families sometimes face include eating disorders, sexual addictions, and gambling.

You need to decide to get help with these problems to improve your life and the lives of those you love. It will make it easier if your partner or spouse supports this decision.

Mental Health Problems

- Mental health problems come in many forms, from anxiety to depression to schizophrenia, and place a great deal of stress on couple and family relationships.
- Depression is particularly common when there are serious relationship problems.
- Having thoughts of suicide is often a sign of depression. Seek help if you struggle with such thoughts.

The good news is that there are now many effective treatments for mental health problems, with services available in all counties, including options for those with limited financial resources.

Domestic Violence

- Although domestic violence can take many forms, *the key is to do whatever is needed to make sure you and your children are safe.*
- Although domestic violence of any sort is wrong and dangerous, experts now recognize that there are at least two very different types:
    - Some couples have arguments that get out of control, with frustration spilling over into pushing, shoving, or slapping. This can be dangerous, especially if you don't take strong measures to stop the patterns from continuing.
    - In other couples, the man uses violence and force to scare and control the woman. Verbal abuse, forced sexual activity, and threats of violence are common. This type of domestic violence is usually the most dangerous and most difficult to change.
- Neither PREP nor this book is a treatment program for domestic violence, although the skills and principles in this book can help some couples manage anger and conflict more safely. Even if you are dealing with a less dangerous pattern of violence in your relationship, you need more help than this book can offer. You might need to seek marital or relationship counseling or the advice of domestic violence experts.
- If you have any questions about the safety of your relationship, you should contact a domestic violence program or hotline, especially if you feel that you are in danger of being harmed.

The bottom line is doing what you need to do to ensure that you and your children are safe. If you ever feel you are in immediate danger from your partner or others, call 911 for help or contact your local domestic violence hotline. There is also a national (U.S.) domestic violence hotline at 800-799-7233.

Where Can I Get More Help?

If you think that you, your partner, or your relationship experiences any of these special problems, we strongly recommend that you get more help. We cannot list local resources for your area in this book, but you can seek help by calling various local agencies or groups, including community mental health centers, a religious organization or religious leader, your physician, substance abuse treatment centers, or private mental health professionals, such as psychologists, psychiatrists, marriage and family therapists, or social workers.

These suggestions were developed by PREP, Inc., with input from the Oklahoma Marriage Initiative. Various experts contributed to the content, including Scott M. Stanley, Howard J. Markman, Theodora Ooms, Natalie H. Jenkins, and Bruce Carruth. Special thanks to Marcia Smith, the executive director of the Oklahoma Coalition Against Domestic Violence and Sexual Assault, for her feedback and recommendations, and to Larry Didier, Prevention Programs Coordinator for the Oklahoma Department of Mental Health and Substance Abuse Services.

RESOURCES AND TRAINING

We have many additional resources available and have included the following section so you can go further if you wish, either as an individual or a couple interested in learning more about how to make a great marriage, or as one who helps couples strengthen their relationships.

Workshops and Training

On our Web site, you can find information about PREP workshops taught by us or by those trained by us in the PREP approach. Go to www.PREPinc.com and click on "Tools for Couples." You can find a directory of workshop leaders in your area by clicking on "Where to find PREP."

We conduct trainings for mental health counselors, clergy, lay leaders, and other marriage educators who desire to be more fully exposed to the PREP approach. For information about these "instructor" workshops, go to www.PREPinc.com and click on "Tools for Leaders," call 303-759-9931, or write to us at the address on the following page. We will be glad to give you information about seminars or products to help you in your own relationship or in your work to help other couples.

Books

In addition to the book you are holding, there are many other titles in this series. You can find out more about these books by calling PREP at 800-366-0166, by calling Jossey-Bass at 415-433-1740, by going online to www.PREPinc.com, or from any bookstore.

Becoming Parents: How to Strengthen Your Marriage as Your Family Grows is the same approach adapted for couples as they become parents. *Empty Nesting: Reinventing Your Marriage When the Kids Leave Home* is the same approach adapted for couples as they enter the empty nest phase.

Fighting for Your African American Marriage teaches the PREP approach while acknowledging the special challenges African American families face.

A Lasting Promise: A Christian Guide to Fighting for Your Marriage is founded on a Christian theological perspective of marriage, and fully integrates that with sound marital research and the strategies of the PREP approach.

Beyond the Chuppah: A Jewish Guide to Happy Marriages is the PREP approach adapted for couples with at least one Jewish partner.

You Paid How Much for That?! How to Win at Money Without Losing at Love teaches couples how to conquer money issues using the PREP approach.

Audiocassettes and Videos

Fighting for Your Marriage audiocassettes and videos are available from PREP Educational Products, Inc. (online at www.PREPinc.com), or they may be ordered from Jossey-Bass. In particular we have a research-driven self-guided video series for couples that teaches some of the key PREP skills and principles.

You can contact us at

PREP
P.O. Box 102530
Denver, CO 80250-2530
E-mail: PREPinc@aol.com
Web site: www.PREPinc.com

Selected Research and References

Amato, P. R., & Booth, A. (1997). *A generation at risk: Growing up in an era of family upheaval.* Cambridge, MA: Harvard University.

Arp, D., & Arp, C. (1997). *Ten great dates to energize your marriage.* Grand Rapids, MI: Zondervan.

Arp, D., Arp, C., Stanley, S. M., Markman, H. J., & Blumberg, S. L. (2001). *Empty nesting: Reinventing your relationship when the kids leave home.* San Francisco: Jossey-Bass.

Baucom, D., & Epstein, N. (1990). *Cognitive behavioral marital therapy.* New York: Brunner/Mazel.

Beach, S. R., & O'Leary, K. D. (1993). Marital discord and dysphoria: For whom does the marital relationship predict depressive symptomatology? *Journal of Social and Personal Relationships, 10,* 405–420.

Buss, D. (2000). *Dangerous passions: Why jealousy is as necessary as love and sex.* New York: Free Press.

Cowan, C. P., & Cowan, P. A. (1992). *When partners become parents: The big life change for couples.* New York: HarperCollins.

Crohn, J., Markman, H. J., Blumberg, S. L., & Levine, J. R. (2001). *Beyond the chuppah: A Jewish guide to happy marriages.* San Francisco: Jossey-Bass.

Cummings, E. M., & Davies, P. (1994). *Children and marital conflict.* New York: Guilford Press.

Doherty, W. J. (2001). *Take back your marriage.* New York: Guilford Press.

Doherty, W. J., Galston, W. A., Glenn, N. D., Gottman, J. M., Markey, B., Markman, H. J., Nock, S., Popenoe, D., Rodriguez, G. G., Sawhill, I. V., Stanley, S. M., Waite, L. J., & Wallerstein, J. S. (2002). *Why marriage matters: Twenty-one conclusions from the social sciences: A report from family scholars.* New York: Institute for American Values.

Fisher, H. (1995). *The anatomy of love: A natural history of mating, marriage and why we stray.* New York: Fawcett.

Forthofer, M. S., Markman, H. J., Cox, M., Stanley, S. M., & Kessler, R. C. (1996). Associations between marital distress and work loss in a national sample. *Journal of Marriage and the Family, 58,* 597–605.

Fowers, B. J. (2000). *Beyond the myth of marital happiness: How embracing the virtues of loyalty, generosity, justice, and courage can strengthen your relationship.* San Francisco: Jossey-Bass.

Fraenkel, P., Markman, H. J., & Stanley, S. M. (1997). The prevention approach to relationship problems. *Sexual and Marital Therapy, 12,* 249–258.

Glass, S., & Strachel, J. (2002). *Not "just friends": Protect your relationship from infidelity and heal the trauma of betrayal.* New York: Free Press.

Glenn, N. D. (1998). The course of marital success and failure in five American ten-year marriage cohorts. *Journal of Marriage and the Family, 60,* 569–576.

Gottman, J. M. (1994). *Why marriages succeed or fail.* New York: Simon & Schuster.

Gottman, J. M., Notarius, C., Gonso, J., & Markman, H. J. (1976). *A couple's guide to communication.* Champaign, IL: Research Press.

Gray, J. (1992). *Men are from Mars, women are from Venus.* New York: HarperCollins.

Grych, J., & Fincham, F. (1990). Marital conflict and children's adjustment. *Psychological Bulletin, 108,* 267–290.

Guerney, B. G., Jr. (1977). *Relationship enhancement: Skill-training programs for therapy, problem prevention, and enrichment.* San Francisco: Jossey-Bass.

Halford, K., & Markman, H. J. (Eds.). (1997). *Clinical handbook of marriage and marital interaction.* London: Wiley.

Halford, K., Markman, H. J., Kline, G., & Stanley, S. M. (forthcoming). Best practices in couple relationship education. *Journal of Marital and Family Therapy.*

Heatherington, M., & Kelly, J. (2002). *For better or for worse: Divorce reconsidered.* New York: Norton.

Holtzworth-Munroe, A., Markman, H. J., O'Leary, D. K., Neidig, P., Leber, D., Heyman, R. E., Hulbert, D., & Smutzler, N. (1995). The need for marital violence prevention efforts: A behavioral cognitive secondary prevention program for engaged and newly married couples. *Applied and Preventive Psychology, 4,* 77–88.

Jacobson, N. S., & Christensen, A. (1998). *Acceptance and change in couple therapy: A therapist's guide to transforming relationships.* New York: Norton.

Jenkins, N. H., Stanley, S. M., Bailey, W. C., & Markman, H. J. (2002). *You paid how much for that?! How to win at money without losing at love.* San Francisco: Jossey-Bass.

Johnson, C. A., Stanley, S. M., Glenn, N. D., Amato, P. A., Nock, S. L., Markman, H. J., & Dion, M. R. (2002). *Marriage in Oklahoma: 2001 baseline statewide survey on marriage and divorce* (S02096 OKDHS). Oklahoma City, OK: Oklahoma Department of Human Services. Available online: okmarriage.org

Johnson, M. P. (1995). Patriarchal terrorism and common couple violence: Two forms of violence against women. *Journal of Marriage and the Family, 57,* 283–294.

Johnson, M. P., Caughlin, J. P., & Huston, T. L. (1999). The tripartite nature of marital commitment: Personal, moral, and structural reasons to stay married. *Journal of Marriage and the Family, 61,* 160–177.

Jordan, P., Stanley, S. M., & Markman, H. J. (1999). *Becoming parents: How to strengthen your marriage as your family grows.* San Francisco: Jossey-Bass.

Karney, B. R., & Bradbury, T. N. (1995). The longitudinal course of marital quality and stability: A review of theory, method, and research. *Psychological Bulletin, 118,* 3–34.

Kiecolt-Glaser, J. K., Malarkey, W. B., Chee, M., Newton, T., Cacioppo, J. T., Mao, H. Y., & Glaser, R. (1993). Negative behavior during marital conflict is associated with immunological down-regulation. *Psychosomatic Medicine, 55,* 395–409.

Kurdek, L. A. (1993). Predicting marital dissolution: A 5-year prospective longitudinal study of newlywed couples. *Journal of Personality and Social Psychology, 64,* 221–242.

Larsen, A. S., & Olson, D. H. (1989). Predicting marital satisfaction using PREPARE: A replication study. *Journal of Marital and Family Therapy, 15,* 311–322.

Levine, J., & Markman, H. J. (2001). *Why do fools fall in love? Understanding the magic, mystery, and meaning of successful relationships.* San Francisco: Jossey-Bass.

Mahoney, A., Pargament, K. I., Jewell, T., Swank, A. B., Scott, E., Emery, E., & Rye, M. (1999). Marriage and the spiritual realm: The role of proximal and distal religious constructs in marital functioning. *Journal of Family Psychology, 13,* 321–338.

Markman, H. J., & Hahlweg, K. (1993). The prediction and prevention of marital distress: An international perspective. *Clinical Psychology Review, 13,* 29–43.

Markman, H. J., Renick, M. J., Floyd, F., Stanley, S. M., & Clements, M. (1993). Preventing marital distress through communication and conflict management training: A four and five year follow-up. *Journal of Consulting and Clinical Psychology, 62,* 1–8.

Markman, H. J., Stanley, S. M., & Kline, G. (forthcoming). Why marriage education can work and how government can be involved: Illustrations from the PREP approach. Conference proceedings. In *Visions 2003: Families over the life course.* From the annual conference of the National Council on Family Relations, Houston, Nov. 2002.

McManus, M. (1993). *Marriage savers.* Grand Rapids, MI: Zondervan.

Miller, S., Wackman, D. B., & Nunnally, E. W. (1976). A communication training program for couples. *Social Casework, 57*(1), 9–18.

Notarius, C., & Markman, H. J. (1993). *We can work it out: Making sense of marital conflict.* New York: Putnam.

Ooms, T. (1998). *Toward more perfect unions: Putting marriage on the public agenda.* Washington, DC: Family Impact Seminar.

Parrott, L., & Parrott, L. (1995). *Saving your marriage before it starts: Seven questions to ask before (and after) you marry.* Grand Rapids, MI: Zondervan.

Pasch, L. A., & Bradbury, T. N. (1998). Social support, conflict, and the development of marital dysfunction. *Journal of Consulting and Clinical Psychology, 66,* 219–230.

Prado, L. M., & Markman, H. J. (1999). Unearthing the seeds of marital distress: What we have learned from married and remarried couples. In M. Cox & J. Brooks-Gunn (Eds.), *Conflict and cohesion in families: Causes and consequences.* Mahwah, NJ: Erlbaum.

Rusbult, C. E., Zembrodt, I. M., & Gunn, L. K. (1982). Exit, voice, loyalty, and neglect: Responses to dissatisfaction in romantic involvement. *Journal of Personality and Social Psychology, 43,* 1230–1242.

Sanders, M. R., Halford, W. K., & Behrens, B. C. (1999). Parental divorce and premarital couple communication. *Journal of Family Psychology, 13,* 60–74.

Silliman, B., Stanley, S. M., Coffin, W., Markman, H. J., & Jordan, P. L. (2002). Preventive interventions for couples. In H. Liddle, D. Santisteban, R. Levant, J. Bray, V. Holt, & R. Levant (Eds.), *Family psychology: Science-based interventions.* Washington, DC: American Psychological Association.

Smalley, G. (1996). *Making love last forever.* Dallas: Word.

Stanley, S. M. (2001). Making the case for premarital education. *Family Relations, 50,* 272–280.

Stanley, S. M., & Fincham, F. D. (2002). The effects of divorce on children. *Couples Research and Therapy Newsletter (AABT-SIG), 8*(1), 7–10.

Stanley, S. M., & Markman, H. J. (1992). Assessing commitment in personal relationships. *Journal of Marriage and the Family, 54,* 595–608.

Stanley, S. M., & Markman, H. J. (1998). Acting on what we know: The hope of prevention. In T. Ooms (Ed.), *Strategies to strengthen marriage: What we know, what we need to know.* Washington, DC: Family Impact Seminar.

Stanley, S. M., Markman, H. J., Prado, L. M., Olmos-Gallo, P. A., Tonelli, L., St. Peters, M., Leber, B. D., Bobulinski, M., Cordova, A. D., & Whitton, S. (2001). Community-based premarital prevention: Clergy and lay leaders on the front lines. *Family Relations, 50,* 67–76.

Stanley, S. M., Markman, H. J., & Whitton, S. (2003). Communication, conflict, and commitment: Insights on the foundations of relationship success from a national survey. *Family Process, 41,* 659–675.

Stanley, S. M., Trathen, D., McCain, S., & Bryan, M. (1998). *A lasting promise: A Christian guide to fighting for your marriage.* San Francisco: Jossey-Bass.

Stanley, S. M., Whitton, S. W., & Markman, H. J. (forthcoming). Maybe I do: Interpersonal commitment and premarital or nonmarital cohabitation. *Journal of Family Issues.*

Sullivan, K. T., & Goldschmidt, D. (2000). Implementation of empirically validated interventions in managed-care settings: The Prevention and Relationship Enhancement Program. *Professional Psychology: Research and Practice, 31,* 216–220.

Waite, L. J., Browning, D., Doherty, W. J., Gallagher, M., Lou, Y., & Stanley, S. M. (2002). *Does divorce make people happy? Findings from a study of unhappy marriages.* New York: Institute for American Values.

Waite, L. J., & Gallagher, M. (2001). *The case for marriage.* New York: Doubleday.

Wallerstein, J. S., Lewis, J. M., & Blakeslee, S. (2000). *The unexpected legacy of divorce: A twenty-five-year landmark study.* New York: Hyperion.

Weiner-Davis, M. (2003). *The sex-starved marriage.* New York: Simon & Schuster.

Weiss, R. L., & Dehle, C. (1994). Cognitive behavioral perspectives on marital conflict. In D. D. Cahn (Ed.), *Conflict in intimate relationships* (pp. 95–115). Mahwah, NJ: Erlbaum.

Whitehead, B. D. (1997). *The divorce culture.* New York: Knopf.

About the Authors

Howard J. Markman, Ph.D., is one of the world's leading experts in the fields of couples research and intervention. He is a professor of psychology at the University of Denver and codirector of the Center for Marital and Family Studies at the University of Denver. He frequently appears in the national media (including the *Oprah Winfrey Show*, the *Today Show*, *20/20*, and *Nightline*) and is invited to give talks on relationships throughout the United States, Europe, and Australia. He is coauthor of the *Fighting for Your Marriage* series and *Why Do Fools Fall in Love?* from Jossey-Bass and coauthor of *The Clinical Handbook of Marriage and Couples Intervention*. He is the codeveloper of the Prevention and Relationship Enhancement Program (PREP) and the author of more than 100 scientific articles, papers, and chapters. Markman also maintains a small private practice in Boulder and Denver, Colorado.

Scott M. Stanley, Ph.D., is codirector of the Center for Marital and Family Studies at the University of Denver, and president of PREP Educational Products, Inc. He has published widely, both research reports as well as writings for couples. He is internationally known for his work on the PREP approach for reducing the risks of marital distress and divorce, as well as his research and theory on marital commitment. Stanley has coauthored the best-selling *Fighting for Your Marriage* book, videos, and audiocassettes. He is also the coauthor of *A Lasting Promise, Becoming Parents, Empty Nesting,* and *You Paid How Much for That?!* from Jossey-Bass. He contributes extensively to both print and broadcast media as an expert on marriage.

Susan L. Blumberg, Ph.D., is a licensed clinical psychologist in part-time private practice in Denver, Colorado, working with children, families, and couples. She is associate director of communications for Developmental Pathways, which serves persons with developmental disabilities and their families. She presents regularly on topics related to communication and conflict management skills to both professional and public audiences. She leads PREP workshops for couples and works with families and organizations interested in improving communication skills. Blumberg has coauthored the best-selling *Fighting* for *Your Marriage* book, videos, and audiocassettes and is a coauthor of *Empty Nesting* and *Beyond the Chuppah*.

NATALIE H. JENKINS is vice president of PREP, Inc., and has been involved in the refinement of the PREP approach for more than 10 years. She has extensive experience in the dissemination of program materials to providers and users of educational services, and oversees product development, training, and marketing for PREP. Jenkins is coauthor of the book *You Paid* How *Much for That?!* and the *Fighting* for *Your Marriage Workbooks*.

CAROL WHITELEY has been a writer and editor in the San Francisco Bay Area for more than 20 years. She is the author of *The Everything Creative Writing Book* (Adams Media, 2002) and the lead author of *Technology, Entrepreneurs, and Silicon Valley* (Institute for the History of Technology, 2002). Her articles, on topics ranging from gift giving to police work, have been published in numerous newspapers, including the *Washington Post,* the *Baltimore Sun,* and the *San Jose / Silicon Valley Business Journal.* She is the cofounder of Writing Doctor (www.writingdoctor.com), an online network providing a range of publishing services to individual and corporate clients.

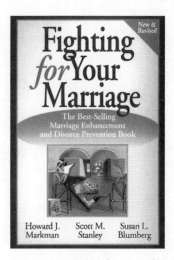

Fighting *for* Your Marriage: Positive Steps for Preventing Divorce and Preserving a Lasting Love (New and Revised)
Howard J. Markman, Scott M. Stanley, Susan L. Blumberg
ISBN: 0-7879-5744-5

"Who said marriages don't come with instructions? *Fighting* for *Your Marriage* takes the guesswork out of creating loving relationships with its powerful and proven program for couples. The valuable new insights included in this edition truly get at the heart and soul of what it takes to make relationships great. Buy this book, read it, and keep it on your nightstand."

—MICHELE WEINER-DAVIS, author of *Divorce Busting: A Revolutionary and Rapid Program for Staying Together*

Since its first publication in 1994, this title has been the best-selling book in its field, providing invaluable, scientifically researched advice on achieving better communication, learning problem solving, understanding commitment, forgiving, restoring intimacy, sharing a core belief system, increasing fun, and improving your sex life. The authors have shown how conflict in intimate relationships is as normal and essential as love. It's how you fight and resolve conflicts that determines the difference between a sustained healthy and satisfying marriage or the pain and frustration of divorce. Nevertheless, continuing research, new clinical fieldwork, and changing cultural and societal attitudes have led to this complete and comprehensive revision of the book, which provides the most up-to-date information, techniques, and guidance for all couples who seek to promote greater character and pleasure in their long-term relationships.

A Lasting Promise: A Christian Guide to *Fighting* for *Your Marriage*

Scott M. Stanley, Daniel Trathen, Savanna McCain, Milt Bryan

ISBN: 0-7879-3983-8

"Finally a practical, easy-to-read book that deals with real marital issues from a Christian perspective! Soundly based on both biblical principles and marital research, *A Lasting Promise* is a must-read for any couple who wants to upgrade their marriage and make it a promise for life!"

—DAVID and CLAUDIA ARP, authors of *The Second Half of Marriage*

This essential resource offers Christian couples a well-researched and proven method for dealing with conflicts and resolving problems in their marriage. *A Lasting Promise* offers solutions to common problems—facing conflicts, problem solving, improving communication, and dealing with core issues—within a religious framework. The strategies outlined can help Christian couples to improve communication, understand commitment, bring more fun into their relationship, and even enhance their sex life.

Becoming Parents: How to Strengthen Your Marriage as Your Family Grows
Pamela L. Jordan, Scott M. Stanley,
Howard J. Markman
ISBN: 0-7879-5552-3

"If you're having a baby, buy this book! It will give your baby the most important gift of all—parents who know how to keep their relationship happy, satisfying, and stable—the kind of relationship your baby can count on and learn from."

—Diane Sollee, director, Coalition for Marriage, Family and Couples
  Education

Moving into parenthood is typically a time of great joy and excitement, but it also brings fatigue, stress, and conflict. From the authors of the best-selling *Fighting for Your Marriage*, this unique and innovative guide offers indispensable advice on how to protect and preserve your marriage and take care of yourselves as you become parents. Based on scientific research and containing real-life examples, *Becoming Parents* challenges you to seize this opportunity to really thrive in your relationship and in parenting together as a team.

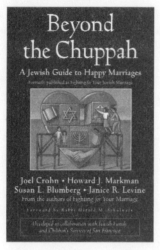

Beyond the Chuppah: A Jewish Guide to Happy Marriages
Joel Crohn, Howard J. Markman, Susan L. Blumberg, Janice R. Levine
ISBN: 0-7879-6042-X

"This much-needed book combines proven research on marital relationships with special insights on Jewish belief systems, making it both culturally sensitive and very sound in terms of what really helps couples save and improve their marriages. For anyone in a Jewish couple, this book is a lifesaver and truly a mitzvah!"

—Celia Jaes Falicov, Ph.D., president, American Family Therapy Academy

Beyond the Chuppah is a hands-on guide for enriching Jewish and interfaith relationships. Based on the proven Prevention and Relationship Enhancement Program (PREP), the book shows couples how to recognize the special issues that are unique to Jewish and interfaith relationships and learn the skills they need to create a marriage that's intimate, loving, and fun. Using the practical tools found in this book, Jewish couples will discover how to "fight right" to resolve conflicts, improve their communication skills, do what's right for the children, and, most of all, appreciate the pleasure of each other's company.

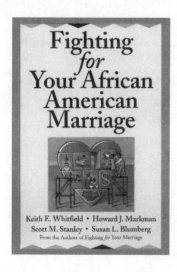

Fighting *for* Your African American Marriage

Keith E. Whitfield, Howard J. Markman, Scott M. Stanley, Susan L. Blumberg

ISBN: 0-7879-5551-5

Fighting for *Your African American Marriage* offers black couples a practical, down-to-earth guide—grounded in more than twenty years of research—that shows what you can do to enhance your marriage, prevent divorce, and put more joy into your life as a couple. The authors show how to cope with the very unique issues of black couples, such as racism, prejudice, discrimination, diversity of background, and tradition within the broad spectrum of their community; different values, rituals, and expectations regarding gender roles; the impact of extended kin and the church; and more. Using the powerful, proven strategies of the highly acclaimed PREP approach, this book helps black couples beat the odds and master the skills that can prevent marital distress and divorce.